THE
MARKETING CHECKLIST

80 Simple Ways to Master Your Marketing

Hank Yuloff

Naked Book Publishing

For Mom and Dad—
They always taught me the importance of doing my best work,
and that stayed with me during the writing.
I wish they were still here to read it!

Contents

The Truth

When it comes to doing business, you should tell the truth all the time. Do not create excuses and don't make promises you cannot keep.

When you are working with clients, the only thing to tell them is the truth. Mark Twain said that "If you tell the truth you have less to remember." Consider the truth as a great and powerful marketing tool.

I put that right up front, because if you are browsing through a bunch of books, trying to decide on which one to buy, even if you do not buy this one, I want to share the most important rule of marketing right at the top.

During my career as a targeted marketing tactician, I have witnessed how people in business make buying decisions in the United States as the economy changes. For established businesses, generating massive sales is not as simple as putting up a sign, inserting an ad in the yellow pages and local newspaper, and joining the Chamber of Commerce (though I highly recommend that last one).

Recently, more and more people have put together scanty, shoestring budgets and opened a business. Sometimes it is a part-time, on-the-side endeavor which they hope grows to full time; other times, they jump right in and make it their main source of income. They have an idea, a brainstorm, a dream, and think people will pay them for their expertise. And it's great expertise, too!

There's a problem, however. They have usually been taught, through classes and experience, to become experts at what they do, but they only have a vague idea of how to tell people about it on a massive scale. Frequently, none of their class work dealt with creating streams of income.

And there is one constant in both cases, none of their competitors want to help them.

The purpose of this book is twofold: To help those entrepreneurs who are just getting started generate income, and to help those entrepreneurs who are well into their business life increase their sales.

We will go through eighty approaches to give you a taste of many marketing methods and in chapter seventy-six you will see a list of over fifty tactics which will help you master your marketing. Using what you learn in this book, you will then have the opportunity to evaluate and score what you are

1

currently doing to market your business and then chart your course of action.

Because you bought this book, you will also have the chance to get help from the OurMarketingGuy.com team by using our Super-Secret web page and e-mail address. We can send you a quick look evaluation and help you to decide your next move.

At the end of each chapter you will find a YES / NO checklist question. It is designed as a way of taking a brief pause so that you can absorb what you have just read and think about how it applies to your company. After you finish the book you will be able to go back and easily see where you may want to get help to easily improve your marketing.

Immediately following the list in chapter seventy-six, you will create a checklist of the marketing tactics you are currently using and see, in one place, what your plan is currently achieving. Of course, if you have a pressing marketing question, you can go to our website, and submit the form to send us an e-mail.

The first six chapters will give you the roadmap we are going to go down together by outlining the basics of your marketing plan.

OK? Let's go to work.

I am going to improve my company's marketing in just 178 pages.
◯ YES ◯ NO

"Three things cannot be long hidden: the sun, the moon, and the truth."
Buddha

"The truth will set you free, but first it will make you miserable."
James A. Garfield

1

The Purpose of a Marketing Plan

Whatever your profession or occupation, there is a learning curve attached to it. You were taught to do what you do, but probably not to market and to sell what you do. It is a rare strategy in a preparatory course that assists the professional in the marketing effort. Talking to people will generate business, but to have a plan—a way of targeting the best clients—is necessary.

The first part of your Marketing Checklist is your marketing plan.

Ask yourself, "Why is my product or service better than the guy next door?" Not having a marketing plan is like opening a restaurant without a menu. It is a road map that is a must for every business.

Here are some things you need to have in your marketing plan:

- The budget
- The targets (demographically or psychographically—who you want to talk to)
- The messages (they will be different for each target)
- The methods (how you will deliver your messages)
- The measurement (how you will decide the effectiveness of each message)

Every part of your checklist is going to relate back to these five essentials elements.

I have a marketing plan that covers these five areas at least minimally.
◯ YES ◯ NO

"The aim of marketing is to know and understand the customer so well the product or service fits him and sells itself."
Peter F. Drucker

2

It All Starts with Budgeting

You have to start with money.

In fact, we all have to start with money. See if this sounds familiar to you: A large percentage of the time, the reason clients do not move forward with working with you is because they lack a budget for your services. They want what you do, but when push comes to shove, they decide that they cannot afford you. The best way to avoid this is to create reasonable expectations from the beginning.

It is the same when you are spending money on your business, and in this case on your marketing. I have found that most companies want to develop more business with expanded marketing efforts, but cash flow is a challenge because they have not planned for it in advance. This is why you need to add marketing as an expense item in your budget. Once you have created your marketing plan, you will be prepared to move forward and implement the plan with a higher rate of success.

I will get to the bottom line right away: If you do not budget for your marketing plan, all of the cool stuff we are going to talk about won't matter; you won't be able to put anything into action, which is just going to cause frustration.

The first question is always, "How do I set up my budget?"

There are two parts to this process. The first is to allocate a percentage of sales for the marketing line item—use about 10% of sales (or 20% of projected sales for a brand new company). Second, you will divide this total among all of the tactics you want to use.

When we added the OurMarketingGuy.com marketing-plan division to our already successful Promotionally Minded promotional products company, we used 30% of projected sales for OurMarketingGuy.com as opposed to 12% of projected sales for the Promotionally Minded part of the company. Promotionally Minded is an established company, but OurMarketingGuy.com was a new brand and was going to have to establish its name in the marketplace. The number is higher for new projects or companies because you have no track record to base it on.

Once you have arrived at your overall number, you will need to break out the specific categories that you will use. Included in this allocated budget will be these basic line items:

- URL registration (about $15)
- Web development (from $500–$2500
- Business card and stationery ($100)
- Networking groups (about $1200 annually each)
- Mailing list development (varies greatly)
- Logo development (about $250–500)
- Copy writing (roughly $50 an hour)
- Promotional products (1000 pens about $500)
- Signage (varies greatly)
- Social media services (it cannot all be done in house!) ($500/month)
- Trade shows (vary widely from a few hundred for a local chamber business expo to many thousands for a multi-day event)
- Ad placement (varies widely)
- You should also plan for price discounts. And lots more possibilities.

There is one more important part of your marketing budget. If budgeting is new to you, add between 5 to 15% cushion for use in things that come up on the spur of the moment. An example of this type of unexpected expense is an ad I included in a competitor's boot-camp workbook that helped me sell my books and develop business which was not in competition to him, but went towards the same target market.

Each business will have different amounts that are appropriate, but this will give you a starting point.

In case you are a bit depressed right off the bat, let me give you an upside to the budgeting process. When you prepare your budget a long time in advance, you often receive discounts for prepayment, or for quantity.

I have prepared a marketing budget.
◯ YES ◯ NO

"And, we have no such thing as a budget anymore.
Our manager freaks when we show him the bill.
We're lavish to the bone, but all our money goes back into the product."
Freddie Mercury

3

What Are Your Client Demographics?

To narrow the field of customers you need to define your customer. The better you can picture your ideal client, the better and more targeted your message will be. Here are some of the individual items which will make up some of that photo:

- Age, sex, height, weight, and sexual orientation
- Marital status (single, married, divorced, widowed)
- Location of their home and office and do they own or rent that home and office?
- Native or foreign born (if foreign, where?)
- Education level achieved and occupation
- Hobbies, musical and entertainment tastes, and where they vacation
- Number of kids and their ages

You will also use these demographic features to communicate differently with each of these generational groups, both in message and technologically: Greatest 1901–1924, Silent 1925–1942, Baby Boomers 1943–1964, Gen X 1965–early 80s, Millennial/Gen Y mid 80s–early 2000s, Gen Z Mid–2000s to today.

In addition, you'll want to know what pain they have that you can solve:

- How often do they need your product?
- Why would they buy from you compared to your competitors?
- Why would they be looking for your product?
- And very importantly . . . do they really *need* your product?

**I have a strong visualization of the demographic features
of my top three clients.**
○ YES ○ NO

---

*"And in the end, it's not the years in your life that count,
it's the life in your years."*
Abraham Lincoln

6

4

Your Targeted Marketing Messages

As I was watching a sporting event on television, my eye was caught by a Just for Men ad. I have grey hair and have pondered doing something about it. In other words, I am in the demographic (forties to seventies, male, and enough disposable income to allow my vanity to affect my wallet) who would use this product. The placement of that ad was easy, from a demographic point of view. It was the content of the ad that surprised me. The models they use in the ad are obviously in their twenties.

Some might ask why is this such a big deal? Beer companies use women in their twenties in beer commercials, don't they? Yes. But the largest demographic of beer drinkers is twenty-one to forty-five. And though men older than forty still enjoy looking at younger members of the opposite sex, they are not going to go along with the subliminal message that if you drink X Brand of beer, you meet sexy women in bikinis. In the case of Just for Men, they should use older male models that their demographic can relate to. Instead, I am left thinking that the man in the ad doesn't have grey hair, the product must not work, and they are trying to hide something.

Your marketing message must not be confusing or allow your target market to think you are excluding them. It must be direct. If you have a visual message, have your models represent your target market in the presentation. In putting together a marketing plan for a client, we always consider the appropriate message based on the demographics of the target market. Sex of the user, age range, occupation, geographic location, income, race, and even sexual orientation can all be factors. Also consider how they spend their disposable income, if they have children, how many children do they have, and what is their educational background.

Remember two things: You want your message to be directed toward your target market and you want to place your message where your target market is looking for them!

I create different messages for different demographic groups.
◯ YES   ◯ NO

"When you aim for perfection, you discover it's a moving target."
George Fisher

5

Methods and Measurement

In my first job out of college I worked for a direct-mail shopper selling display advertisements. Not a slick publication by any stretch of the imagination. It was printed on newsprint and was filled with all advertising. The best areas for this product were in lower income zip codes and my sales territory was in one of the lowest. This meant that my clients generally got a pretty good response.

One day, my boss and I were delivering tear sheets (the one-page sample of their ad) to clients and up next was a neighborhood psychic. When she answered the door, she said she was not going to advertise anymore because it didn't work. Without hesitation, my answer was "You should have known."

When most people hear that story, they think I was commenting on her psychic abilities and that she must not be very good at her business. What I really meant was that for the teeny tiny ad she was running, in a very small geographic area without any kind of a special, there was no way she was going to attain success. I had told her that when we first met.

The point is that prior to entering into any type of marketing activity, whether it is running an ad or exhibiting at a trade show, you have to decide what your measurement of success will be. It could be any number of things: the number of new clients signed up, the number of contacts or sales you make at that trade show booth, or, most often, the dollars generated from a particular method.

At the end of the book, we will discuss several different methods of marketing your business and provide a method of evaluating everything you do.

I have decided on how I will measure my success.
⃝ YES　⃝ NO

"Your brand is formed primarily, not by what your company says about itself, but what the company does."
Jeff Bezos

"Money coming in says I've made the right marketing decisions."
Adam Osborne

6

What in the World Are We Doing Here?

I love doing an exercise during speaking engagements that I call, "What Business Are You In?" It is also one of the very first questions I ask hen during the in-take interview when preparing a marketing plan for a client. I ask, "What business are we in?"

In this exercise, when we go around the table, the answers go something like this: "I'm a lawyer." . . . "I'm an event planner." . . . "I'm a mortgage broker." . . . "I'm a web developer." . . . "I'm an insurance broker."

What they *should* have said was "I solve issues, which provide a level playing field for business." . . . "I transform young peoples' dreams into reality." . . . "I work with the lowest numbers in the industry." . . . "I increase sales with the few clicks of a mouse." . . . "I answer the call when the bell rings in a loss situation, *because I know I am the face of my company and will be the first call.*"

The more you understand what business you are in, and the more time you spend putting it down on paper, the better prepared you will be when customers ask you potential hiring questions.

We also want to know exactly, who is our customer today? Who will our customer be next year? Or, five years from now?

Other questions that we ask when we put together a plan are: What is taking place in our industry that may help you or may hurt you? What technologies are being created that might impact us? How will the future of our industry be different? What trends most threaten our company's continued success? Are we looked at as being innovative in our industry? And is our industry growing or shrinking?

And remember, the big questions are, "Why should they buy from you, and how will they buy from you?

I can easily answer the question "what business are you in?"
◯ YES   ◯ NO

Here is my answer:

_____

_____

_____

_____

_____

_____

_____

_____

"When you reach an obstacle, turn it into an opportunity.
You have the choice. You can overcome and be a winner,
or you can allow it to overcome you and be a loser.
The choice is yours and yours alone. Refuse to throw in the towel.
Go that extra mile that failures refuse to travel.
It is far better to be exhausted from success
than to be rested from failure."
Mary Kay Ash

7

The Three Ways to Offer Your Services and Three Ways to Increase Your Sales

There are three qualities that most clients will want from your product or service. They will want it provided quickly; they expect high quality, and they want it provided at a low price.

At any one time, you will only be able to offer two out of the three. If you aim to deliver all three of these qualities at the same time, you will not be in business very long. In order to provide the product rapidly, your employment and shipping costs will increase. To provide the product with high quality, your raw materials will have to be superior to your competitors. To provide your product at a lower price than your competitors, you will have to find some corners to cut.

With that in mind, there are just three ways you will be able to increase sales:

1. You can sell your products to new customers.
2. You can sell more of that product to current customers.
3. You can sell an increasingly wider product base to current customers.

Sadly, the majority of entrepreneurs will spend the most time on number one, and that is the most expensive way to sell.

So when you are preparing your marketing plans, start with the end in mind—focus on the reason you are sending out your message, and work backwards. At OurMarketingGuy.com we are constantly looking for additional ways to serve our clients.

I constantly look for additional ways to serve my clients.
◯ YES   ◯ NO

---

*"Use what talents you possess; the woods would be very silent
if no birds sang there except those that sang best."*
Henry Van Dyke

8

Hey Buddy, Can You Spare a Dime (on Advertising)?

So there I was, minding my own business at our Chamber of Commerce lunch. It came time for each person to stand up and say who they are and what they do. Pretty standard stuff. And since I knew most everyone in the room, I concentrated a bit more on the faces which were new, because you never know who might need Our Marketing Guy.

One of the new faces was a contractor. He stood up and said that he was the kind of contractor that got invited to his client's weddings and birthday parties. Pretty cool. And then he proudly proclaimed that he had never spent a *dime* on advertising and that all of his work has come to him by word of mouth. That caught my attention pretty quickly.

I thought, Dude, *seriously*? You just spent $350 to join and market your business at the chamber. This past weekend you had a booth at our annual street fair. And as I look at you, I see you are wearing a t-shirt with your logo on it. (And, when I got back to my office, I took a quick look and saw that he had a website, and also found an ad on a merchant site, which may or may not be paid. And that's what I saw before I could do any serious in-depth research.)

So, sir, are you certain you want to keep saying that? It looks like you are spending *a lot* of dimes. (By the way, my office research showed that your digital footprint is *seriously* lacking. If one of those word-of-mouth referrals wanted to check you out, there is not a lot of information to be found outside of your website.)

Ok, Mr. Contractor, look, I understand that you may *think* that "advertising" only includes a print ad in some publication, but if you think you are getting all your business from word of mouth you are not paying attention to what you are doing to *create* that word of mouth.

Just for the heck of it, I sent him a *welcome*-to-the-Chamber-how-can-I-help-you-spread-your-name message. We will see if there is a response.

Are you clear on all of the ways in which you are marketing *your* business? If you don't know—or do not count as part of your marketing strategy—each thing that you do, then you cannot measure it. And if you are not measuring it, then you will not know which marketing strategy to repeat and which to eliminate.

I understand that everything I do, when I am not doing what I do, is marketing.

○ YES   ○ NO

"Half the money I spend on advertising is wasted;
the trouble is I don't know which half."
John Wanamaker

9

Do Not Do Stupid Marketing Stuff

Before we get too far into this book on what you *should* be doing with your marketing, I thought it would be helpful if we discuss some things we should *not* be doing. I realize that most of the time, I'm suggesting that you do things that are smart marketing—change the tags on your videos, add key words to your website, and target some of your markets with direct mail; the list goes on and on.

In this chapter, I am sharing a few things *not* to do, and they all happened to me in one twenty-four hour period while talking to a client at one meeting, and while attending a Chamber of Commerce breakfast.

First, at the meeting, I was talking to a new client who offers IT services to companies. He bounced an idea off of me while we were working on what to add to his promotional products and marketing materials. He said, "When I am in front of a group, I find that I get a lot of attention and laughs when I say 'We take the S*H out of IT.'"

My comment was that if you *really* know your audience well, and you are certain you are not going to anger more than the occasional person, then it is fine. It's funny, smart marketing. But *never* put that in writing. It is similar to one of my elevator speeches for Promotionally Minded Advertising Specialties—I say, "we pollute the world, one t-shirt, calendar, and coffee mug at a time." It always gets smiles and a laugh when I say it at a meeting, but I would never put it on one of our self-promoting pieces.

Now fast forward a few hours to the morning chamber breakfast. Just before the meeting, I was chatting with another business owner that I had seen the previous evening at a networking event. A realtor came up to us and asked where we had been the previous evening. When we told her, she scoffed, held up her hand and said, "*That* place, that is *so* over. I did that." Huh? Telling someone what they are doing in their business, when you have *no* idea how it is working for them is rather, well, . . . insulting. Definitely not smart marketing.

So, the same realtor then sat at my table at the breakfast. She rather loudly pointed out that I, and another table mate, was wearing the name badge on the wrong side of the body (we had them on the left). I asked for an explanation. "Well," she pontificated, "When you shake hands a person's eyes are looking at your right side."

Seriously? Let's bury this one right here. I have heard it before. I'd love to find the self-appointed marketing guru who needed to think up *something* to make his own and that was it. This has to be one of the most stupid things to hold on to as if it was saving your life. My answer? "Ok, then why does every company put their front chest logo on the left side?" Not that *it* matters, either. Personally, I think it is just habit. People that want to meet you will look for your name badge no matter what side it's on. Also, what could she possibly think that she was going to gain from this? Was I going to change my habit? Thank her for giving me a smart marketing tip? Or did she just allow me to cross one realtor off the list of possibilities when we sell our house?

The last thing that happened at this breakfast made the overly-critical realtor look like a genius. The president of the chamber got up in front of the group and announced some joint activities between this chamber of congress organization and three other chambers. His explanation of the cooperative activities included the phrase "we're doing it because the other chambers are smaller and struggling."

Being on the board of one of the partnering chambers (which is neither smaller, nor struggling), I found that remark rather offensive. Some business owners in the room were members of both organizations and this incorrect information might make them think twice about renewing; other members who might consider a dual membership, might not want to join.

The point I am making here is that there are dozens upon dozens of things you should be doing to market your business, but there are hundreds more that you should not be doing. Your job is to be wise enough to know (or hire someone to help you know) the difference.

I won't do stupid stuff.
◯ YES   ◯ NO

"Don't think . . . it hurts the ball club."
Crash Davis, *Bull Durham*

16

10

Sign Up for Social Proof

When clients are considering who to hire, quite often it is the way you set yourself apart that matters. They are looking for tie breakers.

It could be as simple as they like the professional way in which you dress. Or, it could be the amount of preparation you did prior to your meeting. It could even be that you answered a question by saying, "You know, I do not know the answer. I will check and get you an answer." It is never good to guess, especially if you have no idea. These are all ways of developing a positive image. In current parlance, this is called *social proof.*

In the case of our corporate name—Promotionally Minded, and increasingly in our marketing-plan brand name—OurMarketingGuy.com, we have been very involved in our communities. We are members of several chambers of commerce. I have been involved with local politics, and have received a number of awards for this involvement, including several for volunteerism.

It costs money. It costs time. It takes a desire to be involved in your community. But, in my rarely to be humble opinion, a company that does not give back, a company that does not "get it" (that it is their community that supports them) will have a harder time making it.

Our local chamber, EncinoChamber.org, has held a street fair for twenty-seven years called The Taste of Encino. When given the opportunity, I buy a street banner that announces the event and carries my company name. The banners that promote the event were up for a month prior to it on the main thoroughfare in the area. And the cool thing is I have had people say that they saw our name on the banners and were convinced that we were a major sponsor of the event! Pretty awesome.

I also use photos of that banner all the time to promote what we do in the community. One of those photos was used as part of a collage for the 2015 chamber directory—extra social proof for our company.

I am always generating social proof.
◯ YES ◯ NO

"Giving back involves a certain amount of giving up."
Colin Powell

11

Signs and Location

Business does not arrive just because you put a sign in the window. But if you are going to have a retail store, you are going to need one. Large, easy to read signage is very important. Don't be fancy. Just be clear. When you design the logo for your retail space, keep in mind that people—your new customers—will be looking for you as they drive and you want them to be able to find you easily. Who wants an angry customer? Look at the signage for some of the largest companies especially gas stations and fast food chains. Let these be a guide when you are designing your signs.

Color makes a difference as well. There is a reason that stop signs are red with white lettering—it is the easiest to read. Warning signs are yellow with black lettering because they are second most important. Don't let this be your only decision in choosing a logo and company colors, but you should know about it. My company logo colors? Red, white, and black.

Good location is vital. Obviously you want to avoid paying the highest rent in the area, unless you own the market and an awesome product. It is very advantageous to be by a business that generates a lot of traffic, especially if your products complement the other businesses. All this, plus plenty of free parking will go a long way to ensure your success.

The clients of our promotional products (through PromotionallyMinded. com) know that their advertising has now become a sign on their customers' desks. Inexpensive signs that scream their name all day long.

I have incredible signage.
◯ YES ◯ NO

"A business with no sign is a sign of no business."
Merritt Robinson

"I never thought I'd be successful.
It seems in my own mind that in everything I've undertaken
I've never quite made the mark.
But I've always been able to put disappointments aside.
Success isn't about the end result;
it's about what you learn along the way."
Vera Wang

Four Ways to Time the Delivery of Your Marketing Message

Twice a year Our Marketing Guy (a division of Promotionally Minded) puts on a two-day marketing boot camp. It is a day when we invite all our clients, and a lot of companies we *want* to have as clients, to improve their marketing acumen. For our September show, our first mailings to clients went out in the middle of July. We added promotional flyers to each website front page and began talking about it at chamber and networking meetings.

Why the middle of July? Timing. It makes no sense to tell people about the show any earlier because we found out by surveying our clients that sixty days was the appropriate time to let them know about it. Before that it is too early for them to lock it into their calendars. (We also tell people on our blog to fill in a form that we put at the bottom of each entry.)

Timing is very important to your marketing message. In our blog, we quite often discuss current event marketing, where you take something that is going on in the news and use it to market your business. Here are four examples:

1. In the months leading up to a major election, it is great to use a vote-for-me theme in your marketing. People are used to seeing election ads and easily understand that you are asking them to vote for you by purchasing your services. That same ad has a much lower response rate when we are not in an election season.

2. It can be great to tie your message into a calendar event and time of year. Auto dealers are notorious for insert-the-holiday-here ads. In my opinion, you run the risk of people not believing your message if you do it too often, but when used sparingly ("Our annual Arbor-day sale" for a paper company would be a good example) it is effective. We only run one annual marketing show with the specials that go with it. Similarly, in the video attached to our blog, I was at a Lake Tahoe ski resort during the summer which is not the right time to talk about skiing.

3. Use the major anniversaries of your business. Five, ten, twenty, twenty-five and on are causes to celebrate. Many companies tie a discount to that number to make it more memorable ("An extra 5% off," or "10% extra product to celebrate our 10th anniversary" or "50% off your meal on the date of our 50th anniversary").

4. We have one retail client that gives out "company dollars" which are good on one special date. For two months they give out these company dollars with each sale, telling customers to hold on to those dollars and on the target day, redeem them. Remember: make your message easy to remember by tying it to a larger-than-you event.

I am always looking for new and improved ways to time the delivery of our marketing messages.
○ YES ○ NO

---

*"Strategy and timing are the Himalayas of marketing.
Everything else is the Catskills."*
Al Ries

"If you do things well, do them better. Be daring, be first, be different, be just."
Anita Roddick

13

Are You Guarantying Your Warranty?

In Los Angeles there's a mattress store that for years has said that they can beat any store's advertised price or your mattress is "Freeeeee."

The tone of voice used by the owner of the company who does these ads is quite obnoxious but it has stuck in the minds of those in the area. And the company seems to back up their promise because with the amount of advertising they do, we would hear about it in Los Angeles.

Can you back up the product you are selling for a period of time with a warranty or guaranty? If you are going to say it, you better be able to back it up because in the information age people who feel they have been done wrong have innumerable places on the Internet to let the world know.

We offer two guarantys in our company: With PromotionallyMinded. com we say that if a client is not happy with their promotional products, we make it right. Period. This came from the years when I worked for a competitor. If something went wrong with an order, it sometimes seemed like it took an act of Congress to make it right for the client. I decided that this would be one of our unique selling propositions.

Our second guaranty is for a marketing boot camp we hold twice a year. One of the ways we promote it is with our Five-Star Guaranty (TheFive-StarSeminar.com). Simply stated it goes like this: Remember when you were in school and there was something very important in your notes? You would add a star or some other mark. Well, we say that you will star at least five marketing tools, tactics, or ideas in your workshop notes. If you don't, we will refund your money at the end of the day.

Prior to publication of this book, I have only issued one refund, to Scott Freedman of www.Visirity.com. Why did I mention him? So that anyone can check out our guaranty for themselves, *and* I want to promote him. If I can get him enough business, he may want to come to another of our events, and I will get another chance at helping his business improve.

My company is so good, it unconditionally guarantys its work.
○ YES ○ NO

*"Success is neither magical nor mysterious. Success is the natural consequence
of consistently applying the basic fundamentals."*
Jim Rohn

*"Above all, you want to create something you are proud of.
That's always been my philosophy of business.
I can honestly say that I have never gone into any business
purely to make money.
If that is the sole motive,
then I believe you are better off doing nothing."*
Richard Branson

*'When you come to the Our Marketing Guy Marketing Boot Camp,
you receive the Five-Star Guarantee.
If you do not 'star' five immediate game changers,
you get your money back at the end of the day."*
Hank Yuloff

24

14

The Right Tools, the Right People

I saw this post on Facebook: "I have an HTM webpage I created in word. When trying to export to an e-mail, I'm either losing the images altogether, or they are shrinking and not holding up the table width. How do I save an HTM to be able to send as an e-mail newsletter?"

I appreciate the concept that you want to do things yourself. I know I sure do. Technology has made many functions a lot easier. But just as we don't use a screwdriver to hammer a nail, we need to use the correct technology in the right way.

In this case, my personal-trainer friend who posted that can write her own information to turn into an e-mail, but then she should either learn the right way to put the e-mail together, or hire someone who knows what they are doing. In the long run it will save you time, which saves you money. You will also like the look of your marketing materials much more if you do.

There are right ways and wrong ways to do things; choose the right way.

I have put together a team that can get things done faster than I can do them myself.
◯ YES ◯ NO

"Well begun is half done."
Aristotle

"If you don't have time to do it right, when will you have time to do it over?"
John Wooden

Repeat Over and Over, Referrals Are the Best Source of My Business

On the other side of that line, always be a good source of referrals for your clients and other business people. Support other business owners as much as you can, it's *not* all about your business (you gotta give to receive!). One of the best things about my business is the size of my referral base. I have made it a point to get to know lots of business people in various industries so I can be seen as a connector. I strive to be the go-to guy for my clients when they need a referral or want to be referred.

Train yourself to listen to business conversations. When someone has an issue, think "Who do I know that can solve that?"

Those four words are important to memorize: Who do I know? They work when you are asking for referrals (example, an insurance agent may ask, "Who do you know that just got married?" if they are looking to sell life insurance) or when you are giving them.

There are lots of business networking groups, which we will talk about in the next chapter, that can be a great source of these referrals, but you must learn their proper "care and feeding."

While we're on the subject of referral business, how are you taking care of, nurturing, and showing appreciation to your referral sources?

I make a point of mailing a handwritten card using our online greeting card system (www.CardsByHank.com). We create the cards online and a service we use, prints, stuffs, stamps and mails them. I feel they work to generate more referrals because I know how I feel when I receive a card for doing the same thing. Find the appropriate method for your industry to send thank yous.

I reward my referrals.
◯ YES   ◯ NO

"Success is a lousy teacher. It seduces smart people into thinking they can't lose."
Bill Gates

16

The Power of Groups

At every stage of my business career I have been a member of business networking groups.

If you just started your business and after working for someone else have gone out on your own, these groups can be an immediate boost to your sales. If you work for someone else as a sales rep, they can become extensions of your own sales efforts. If your business is more mature, they are great for inexpensively re-igniting yourself to go out and get new business.

There are dozens of these groups available, and they come in a few different types. First there are industry groups, which are dedicated to building the image and education of their members. Networking within these groups is great because of the inside know how you can generate. Within the promotional product industry, I am a past president of one of these groups, and have found that the relationships I built there have helped my business in many ways, such as expedited service in an "advertising emergency."

Next, there are the soft networking groups. I prefer chambers of commerce, because I feel that being involved in the communities you do business in is very important. It helps you know what is going on in your area and you become seen as a local expert. I also suggest that you join the chamber ambassador committee. They are the meeters and greeters and under that designation you can call any chamber member to develop a friendship and to "keep them up to date" on chamber activities.

There are also hard networking groups which meet weekly with the specific purpose of learning about the businesses within the group so you can actively and constantly pass referrals. I have found that in one of these groups, there needs to be over twenty-five, and preferably over thirty members for the group to hit a critical mass of leads being passed around. When visiting these groups you will likely hear a lot of hype about how good they are. Make sure you visit three times before making a commitment so that you get a very good feeling for how strong the particular group is. If you don't get a great feeling, move on and try another. You are making an every week, year-long commitment and it had better be worth it. It's also important for you to decide what your breakeven point is, which includes time spent. For most businesses that number is $4000 in revenue for each $1000 spent (lawyers, advertising specialists, florists, and other companies that have a product). For most service businesses, the rule of thumb drops a bit to $3000.

These groups usually will give each person a chance to stand up and say what they do, and help you learn the proper way to give your elevator speech. Remember in your message to paint word pictures for your audience. An example: "A good lead for me is one of your business owner friends who is heading for a trade show. We have ways to keep their booth so busy they won't have a chance to realize how much their feet hurt." Another example: "In the television show M*A*S*H, Colonel Potter had Corporal Radar O'Reilly to keep his unit running. Many times, Radar knew what forms Potter would need before *Potter* knew he needed it. Every business owner you know that has an office staff occasionally needs a Radar as temporary help for a project or to just answer their phones perfectly, but remotely. Our virtual assistant company is *your* Radar."

Don't make the mistake of trying to reinvent the wheel by starting your own group. Many people don't like the rules of a group and think they can do a better job of putting together a networking group built on their own networking expertise, as a way to pass leads. I understand that it is a great thing to say it's a group that you put together, but it is going to take a lot of your time and effort and that is usually time much better spent on building your business. It is far better to just plug yourself into some group's system and be one of the cogs, making it work. *System*, after all, stands for Save Yourself Some Time Effort and Money!

I utilize the power of groups to build my business.
◯ YES ◯ NO

"The power of one, if fearless and focused, is formidable,
but the power of many working together is better."
Gloria Macapagal Arroyo

17

Being Prepared for Emergency Situations

As hurricane Sandy bore down on the USA, there were things many companies did that was of great community assistance, and which in the long run, helped their public image. In the promotional product industry for example, our national organization sent out an e-mail listing what over thirty factories on the East Coast were doing operationally; most were closed. This helped everyone nationally know when to expect their orders would go out, or to know that at that moment, they should not call, but rather use web sites for information gathering. That e-mail also gave information on how we could assist those challenged companies. This showed a proper level of leadership for the industry. And it is not the first time that our industry has rallied in this way. *So*, what is *your* plan?

Depending upon your industry, it may be a good opportunity to proactively let your clients know how you would be able to continue to serve their needs, or how your service may be effected, in the case of a natural disaster. It should be a part of your public relations plan, one of several in a binder filled with emergency plans. This should be available to be referenced by all employees and put into action if, say, something happens while management is on vacation.

Here are some things you need to address:
- How is your computer network backed up?
- How can it be accessed in case of emergency?
- Do you have alternate phone numbers that can be used?
- Is there a backup location where your staff can meet?
- In what order does current work get triaged for importance?
- How is everyone going to get their paycheck!!!?

Before you find yourself in a dangerous situation, it might be a good idea to prepare e-mails to your clients, letting them know you have a plan to service their needs. Staying in contact is *always* good customer service, and therefore, a good marketing goal.

I have a plan to be up and running immediately after an emergency.
○ YES ○ NO

"Be Prepared."
Motto of the Boy Scouts of America (well, that and,
"Why use a flint and stone when you have matches?")

18

The E-mail That Hinders More Than Helps

In a recent email, I received this follow up from someone I had seen the night before:

> "Hello Hank,
>
> It was nice seeing you recently.
>
> It would be my pleasure to assist you or anyone you care about that needs help with a (name of industry) transaction anywhere in the United States since (name of his company) is a national company. I look forward to talking with you soon.
>
> Best Regards,
>
> 'His contact info'"

I have not changed anything in the email. This is exactly as I received it. It's not the worst follow up I have gotten, but it certainly is not very personal. And it would not score any points if you sent this message inappropriately. Here is why: The sender of this e-mail and I have done business together in the past. We see each other *all* the time at chamber functions. Although we had not seen each other very much recently, we had seen each other that very night. What this e-mail says to me is that I just got the equivalent of an e-mail *form letter*.

It's completely all right to use programs that "mail merge" the information of several people into the same letter. Automation plays a very important part in marketing. But if you are going to use this tool, make certain that it is used appropriately. Otherwise you will not look very savvy. It is possible that you may have to create several different letters for various lists of potential clients.

You also have to remember that your goal is to build and improve a relationship with the other person. If you make it impersonal (showing that you do not pay attention to them as an individual), or too salesy, you will be doing the exact opposite. Our company logo is a *target* . . . I constantly try and remind my clients that they have many different targets for their message. But they have to treat each as a separate target and mold the message to the specific target; and complete it!

When I use e-mail services, I am going to use them the right way.
◯ YES   ◯ NO

"I am certainly not one of those who need to be prodded.
In fact, if anything, I am the prod."
Winston Churchill

"If you're not a risk taker, you should get the hell out of business."
Ray Kroc

19

Your E-mail Address Should Promote You

I recently got off the phone with a headhunter; he (giggle) wanted me to go to work for *someone else* (snicker) in the promotional product business—boy does he have *that* wrong. He had called before and is a genuinely nice man so I gave him a few minutes to talk shop about the promotional product business. We made plans to chat in the new year about some marketing ideas (he *needs* a couple of the tools I use to stay in touch with potential clients).

Anyway, he sent me a follow up e-mail from a sbcglobal.net e-mail address—*no, no, no!* If you are a professional, use your own company e-mail address. Even if you only use your website as a brochure, you should have one. In this case, he does not have a website (yeah, yeah I will work on him) and I think that is making him work harder than he needs to.

What is worse, he is selling himself to *marketing professionals* who would never use those addresses as their primary e-mail address. It is the same as not having a mailing address on your business card.

There is a place for a generic e-mail addresses but *not* in business. You can use them for all the "free information" sites you go to.

In my response e-mail, I suggested to him that he needs to hire OurMarketingGuy.com. We will get him to begin using sales funnels and a CRM (customer relationship management) system that will help him keep track of the five hundred plus bodies he is trying to sell into the captivity of a boss. But that is for another day.

This can be boiled down to one word: *professionalism.*

When I talk to business decision makers, the same thing keeps coming up, if you are using an AOL, Yahoo, SBCGlobal, etc. e-mail address, you will be looked at as if you are a part time business. Your credibility score is going to take a hit, no matter how good you are at your business. You need to do yourself a favor; go buy a domain name that ties into your business and set up your e-mail address in a professional manner. It sends the wrong message to use this type of e-mail addresses; it's as if your business is not real, and it looks like spam.

Also, why would you want to advertise Yahoo or Gmail or SBCGlobal instead of yourself?

I am never, never, never, never, ever going to argue with Hank Yuloff about the way to select an e-mail address. He is right.

○ YES   ○ NO

"I do love e-mail. Wherever possible I try to communicate asynchronously. I'm really good at e-mail."
Elon Musk

"It has been my observation that most people get ahead during the time that others waste."
Henry Ford

"In my opinion, people who use e-mail addresses that are not based on their company websites are screaming that they are unprofessional part-timers who don't fully believe in what they are doing."
Hank Yuloff

20

Four Words That Can Cost You Business

For every order of promotional products we get at Promotionally Minded, we make a follow up call to check on the production progress. I was surprised the other day when I got this answer to the length of time it was taking to produce the order: "That question is not in my area, you need to call back and contact Mrs. X in the art department." Huh? What do you mean it is not your job? Just like my clients should see me as the one-stop shop for answers, anyone in your company who receives a client question should either have the point person get back to your client or they should get the answer for them.

This came right after an incident I had at a hospital regarding the move of a family member from one department to another. I received one set of instructions from someone in the first department. But when it came time to execute the move, it turned out that another department had also given instructions for the move; two different departments had written checks for the move. But a third department—the logistics department—would not cash either check. They were very clear that "it's not my job and there is no way I will work with you to make this happen."

I am not saying that we need to follow the mantra that the customer is always right; they clearly are not. But there is usually a way to make the customer feel special.

There is a dentist I worked with recently that was looking for a way to convert potential clients into butts in his chair. Literally. When calls came in, the receptionist was answering the "How much will it cost to ___" questions with, "I don't know," or, "I will have to take a message." That verbiage has now been changed to, "It sounds like you may be in pain. Would you like to speak to the doctor?" A change in words causes a change in attitude by the customer. In this case, the dentist is converting many more phone calls into patients.

This was an employee training issue. One of the things that we do when we produce a marketing plan for businesses is to train employees to understand that customers pay their salary. They also have to be empowered to try and solve customer issues, and taught to never say, "that's not my job." If you want your customer service to be given a jump start, avoid those four little words that show you do not care.

Important point: When you empower your employees to solve a client issue on the spot, you have to stand behind them. If they make a mistake in solving it, you can use it as a training and growth exercise for the company. Congratulate the employee for taking initiative—"I'm proud of you. Thanks for taking care of our clients. Next time that happens, can we do ____ or ____ instead?" Then calmly explain why. But for one last time, you should thank the employee for doing something good.

**It is my company, and therefore everything is my job
because the buck stops with me.**
◯ YES   ◯ NO

---

*"I hate comics that try to change the world. That's not my job.
That's for the king. I'm the jester. I'm there to make you laugh."*
Ralphie May

36

21

Hold on a Sec

In my business, sometimes I am placed on hold. This chapter is here because of a call that began with me being placed—automatically—on hold for twelve minutes and forty-nine seconds. I then asked to speak to the object of my affection and was told . . . , "Hold on a sec."

Let's back up a bit.

Sometimes, being on hold is not a useless thing. It can even be an opportunity for the company placing you on hold, if they make it worth your time. Either play some rockin' music or better yet, give some good and creative information, such as:

- Provide an announcement of some new products.
- Tell a story which will help you sell more of your product .
- Choose an option for silence.
- Provide a set period when you will call people back "We return all calls between 11 a.m. and noon, and between 5 and 6 p.m." Leave this as your message.
- Give them the option of leaving a message and tell them you will call them right back. But then: *call them right back* within a very reasonable amount of time.
- How about giving a special code word, "When we come on to the line, say the word 'Constantinople' and receive 10% off our new XYZ."

They called you for a reason; you have an opportunity to flex your marketing muscles.

Here are three things I would not do:

1. I would not use a radio station because you are then advertising the station instead of your business and if the receiver gets bumped, your customers will be treated to a lot of annoying static.
2. Do not use, "Your call is very important to us. We will be right back to you." If my call was *that* important, you would have a live receptionist answer my call.
3. For goodness sake, do not use, "Please pay attention as our options

have changed." No, they have not. You just want people to take less time with your receptionist; and it doesn't matter anyway, each call is a new experience—it doesn't matter what you did in the past. And as long as I am ranting here, why *are* you really recording the conversations for training purposes?

These are people who want to do business with you. They deserve your undivided attention.

The end of my phone story? The guy came back on the phone three minutes later and said that she was not in. When I asked if I could leave a message, he said, "Oh, yeah, here."

The call was then disconnected.

We strive to never put someone on hold.
◯ YES ◯ NO

"Most of what we call management consists of making it difficult for people to get their work done."
Peter Drucker

"Time is your most important resource. You can do so much in ten minutes. Ten minutes; once gone is gone for good."
Ingvar Kamprad

22

Your Call Is Very Important to Me

Have you dialed your cell phone lately? Or your office line? Let me ask you: Based on what you heard on the voice mail, would you do business with you? Here are a few tips:

- Smile when you record your message. It will show through.

- Practice your message using the memo feature of your phone. Record your message, listen to it, and then improve it in your next recording. Repeat until it sounds just the way you want it to.

- Get it done quickly—once people are disappointed that they have gotten voice mail, they know what to do; get to the important point and let us hear that beep.

- There are some people who use their voice mail as a way to deliver important information. For example, there are mortgage brokers who update their voicemail every day with the current rate. They have trained real estate agents to call them.

- This brings us to another point: I know some people who never answer their phones. They say it disturbs their work flow. I understand but generally disagree with this, but if this is you, set regular times when you return calls and include that in your voice mail message: "I check messages regularly and will return your call by (at) the end of business today." Just make certain you do it.

I have a spectacular and creative voice mail message.
◯ YES ◯ NO

"I see people putting text messages on the phone or computer and I think, '
Why don't you just call?'"
William Shatner

"If you want a free e-mail service that doesn't use your words
to target ads to you, you'll have to figure out how to port
years and years of Gmail messages somewhere else,
which is about as easy as developing your own free e-mail service."
Al Franken

23

Who May I Say Is Calling?
(Clue: She Is Not In)

The way your office phone is answered can make a big difference in how the company is viewed. You never know who may be calling you to give you a lead, but is first checking on some detail before wasting your time in case it is not a good match.

We put together a marketing plan for a family-law attorney in Glendale, California. I thought we had a good relationship, so I let my usual payment schedule lag, and before I knew it she owed us a decent amount of money. It was at that point she ended the relationship.

When I would make a collection call, her receptionist would ask who was on the line. I would reply, "Hank Yuloff. Is she in the office?"

"Yes. One moment please." Then, after twenty seconds I would either be dumped into voicemail without the receptionist coming back on the line, or she would say that the lawyer was not in. I decided that this lawyer was behaving unprofessionally and needed to go to collections.

The point here is that you may not be a deadbeat family-law attorney in Glendale, California avoiding the call of someone to whom you owe money; you may just be very busy and not want to take calls from a salesperson or anyone else while you take care of work. If that is the case, your front line people who answer the phone must be honest and *before knowing* who is on the line say that you are in the office but asked that anyone who calls understand that you will take a break at 3 p.m. and return a call to them at that time. Then return *all* of the calls.

Train your staff to know that you do not know who is calling to bring you business and how the call is handled from the very beginning could make a difference in your bottom line.

I have secret shopped my own office.
◯ YES   ◯ NO

"Why give in to rudeness, when you can fight back with kindness."
Donna A. Favors

41

24

Searching for the Marketing Silver Bullet

Every salesperson I ever met for every type of advertising, marketing, online or offline promotional product or method believes that they are selling the one best product that you need. They will each tell you that it will solve all your marketing problems. That is because they live on commissions.

My opinion has always been that if they cannot easily rattle off a list of business types that they cannot help, they do not know their product well enough and are not confident enough in it to market it to you. There is no "silver bullet" of advertising which will be the magical answer to all your sales prayers. I know this because early in my career, I sold daily newspaper advertising, direct mail advertising, promotional products, and weekly shopper advertising.

I would tend to be wary of buying from an advertising salesperson that is in their first year working for a company. They need to have gotten through an entire yearly cycle. Also, if they have not been through a year, then you do not know if they have a solid track record of success.

This has been especially true in the last few years with the onslaught of technological products where measuring their effectiveness is difficult. I would suggest that you ask them for the names of several clients in similar industries who can tell you that the product works and works well.

I have heard many salespeople selling search engine optimization services where they claim they can get your business on the front page of "fill in the blank search engine." This is faulty for two reasons. First, search engines do *not* make special deals with companies to put their clients on the front page. Second, anyone can get on the front page of the search engines for their company name. For example, if someone types in "promotionally minded promotional products" they will be delivered to my company home page. But if they just type in promotional products, they will probably not unless they include a location tag—Encino, California, or Los Angeles, California, or San Fernando Valley, California.

For your company to be successful, you should be using several avenues of marketing. Use a variety of online methods: website, social media, pay per clicks, mobile apps, etc. Use diverse offline methods: traditional advertising (broadcast and print), direct mail, personal networking to name but a very few. You should have each one back up the other, and use consistent messages throughout.

I am using more than five methods of marketing my business and I am regularly measuring their effectiveness.
○ YES   ○ NO

"Every crowd has a silver lining."
PT Barnum

"Every silver lining has a touch of grey."
Jerry Garcia

"People that think they have found a silver bullet for their marketing because they are doing one thing that is working;
that is all they have to do now and in the future.
They also buy magic beans
and think that they will bring them the golden goose.
But you know what you get with geese?
Goose droppings."
Hank Yuloff

25

Keeping Clients in the Loop, Sharing Good News

I believe that my clients are extremely important to my success. When something excellent happens in Our Marketing Guy or Promotionally Minded, it has everything to do with their involvement. It is all very symbiotic.

Once when I was on the North Shore of Oahu in Hawaii on vacation, I noticed something that struck an odd chord. For those who do not know the area, a common restaurant model is "The Hawaiian Shrimp Truck." This is usually some sort of school bus or UPS delivery van that has been changed into a rolling kitchen.

We saw one truck with a huge "Under New Management" banner across the entire side of it. Because of the age of the truck, I must say I was skeptical.

Turns out, they were telling the truth! They had purchased the truck about ninety days ago and were just starting to build their shrimp selling empire! By displaying that banner they are doing exactly what they *should* be doing to promote their business. If I go back there a year from now and still see that banner, then we have a whole new discussion, but for now—*shrimp on!*

So what is new in *your* business? And are you telling your clients about it? If you have a new product or service what better way to promote it than with a press release to the appropriate new media, or if you have some new staff members send a letter to your clients. If you just won an award you should be telling *everyone*, especially your clients. And, all of this should be part of your blog!

On that note, I would like to proudly announce that I, Hank Yuloff, was just selected Employee of the Month for Promotionally Minded for over 220 straight months. Every year, I mail my clients a greeting card using the www. CardsByHank.com system that announces that happy fact. I put it in the form of a newspaper article that gives the highlights of the year. For example, in the 2015 card, clients will get the news that we have an upcoming weekly radio show and have expanded the Promotionally Minded Marketing Days to twice a year.

One of the most important factors in sharing the good news, is that when you are spreading the news, it is a non-sales reason to talk to your clients. This develops a relationship that is not completely dependent on business and gives you another opportunity to show appreciation to your clients.

When you hear of a client who has some good news about themselves—an award or anything positive, really, it is a great opportunity to congratulate them and promote it on your social media page. Build that relationship.

**Our company shares good news with clients and public venues
that are important to our company.**
○ YES ○ NO

---

*"There is good news from Washington today.
Congress is deadlocked and can't act.*
Will Rogers

*"First the doctor told me the good news.
I was going to have a disease named after me."*
Steve Martin

26

Finding Hidden Gems
in Your Marketing Draft

I love baseball season, so I thought I would use an appropriate metaphor to help you visualize a marketing point.

Ruth, DiMaggio, Yastrzemski, Bonds, Mays, Maddox, Aaron—there are some names that would garner attention in the Major League Baseball draft because of the pedigree of that player namesake. From a marketing point of view, it would be a grand slam to post a photo along with a blog about the player. It's the same with some of our own products and services; the ones that are easy to promote because they are our main sellers. Sometimes there are products and/or targeted markets that lay within our grasp and we just have to take a look around to find them.

In this case, let's take the Boston Red Sox: The Beantown nine play at a field called Fenway Park. It's a one hundred years old and considered to be a gem of a ball field. If the marketing department were allowed to decide who the team would draft to come up through the ranks, the high school ball-player they would be drafting is in Boca Raton Florida and has a very familiar name. Last name is Parks, and his first name is the same as my cat—Fenway. Yep, Fenway Parks could be be playing at Fenway Park.

In the marketing department, we do not make a bad product sell; we draw attention to and make a good product sell better. We look for the angels and messages that will highlight the benefits to our clients when using our products and services. Using my company as an example, there are very few people in the promotional products industry who hold a Certified Advertising Specialist designation (about 10%). There are even fewer who have their college degrees in advertising and public relations. So when developing the Our Marketing Guy division of Promotionally Minded, it was easy to develop programs that would benefit our clients in ways far beyond selling them trade show giveaways. Most people in my business—my competitors, when asked why they are special say they have great prices and great service. I have witnessed it twice a week at two different Chamber of Commerce meetings. What do *your* competitors say?

More importantly, who is *your* Fenway Parks? What products are your clients *used* to getting from you that they could also get from competitors?

There must be reasons that they get them from you. So ask them what you do differently than your competitors that keeps them coming back to you. It is your heat, your Fenway Parks.

**I am on the lookout for new ways
to differentiate myself from competitors.**
○ YES   ○ NO

---

*"Good business leaders create a vision, articulate the vision,
passionately own the vision, and relentlessly drive it to completion."*
Jack Welch

"My own business always bored me to death; I prefer other people's."
Oscar Wilde

Google Hangouts,
a Multi-use Marketing Tool

When I speak in public on various marketing topics, I have begun to ask two questions: "Who has heard of Skype?" Every hand goes up. Then I ask, "Who has heard of Google Hangouts?"

The number of raised hands drops to about 10%.

Simply put, Google Hangouts (GHO) are the Google+ version of a live video chat product with several great features. You can include up to nine people on them, which is great for holding private meetings. Each of those participants can be in their own office and use the webcam and microphone on their computer. This saves travel time for everyone.

You can also use it to broadcast a live event to a public audience. Picture a sales meeting for one hundred remote salespeople where they each log on to a YouTube account, and up to nine people (sales managers, sales support personnel) can have a speaking part in the meeting. The one hundred salespeople can type in questions to the leader of the GHO.

Imagine, also, holding a monthly lecture series for your clients on topics that are important to them where you do not have to rent a hotel meeting room and you can include a world-wide audience instead of just local invitees. Your clients have the advantage of getting information without having to leave their office. No traffic? You just scored lots of points. Another great benefit is that for these conferences, you no longer have to hire a videographer because a GHO is recorded by your computer and is immediately uploaded to the hangout initiator's YouTube account.

You can also do one-on-one training with a client using GHOs and record the session. The client can then go back and review it. Some of my clients that are doing this, offer the service for a bit more money.

Lately, I have begun using the GHO as a way to promote my clients. I interview them for about fifteen minutes, which creates a permanent web presence for them to use as a promotional video. All they have to do is go to my YouTube channel, grab the embed code and attach it to an e-mail. An additional tool that makes the GHO even more effective is when I add a web form that is connected to my Customer Relationship Manager (CRM) so that when someone views the video and wants more information, they can easily obtain it by filling out the form. When a lead comes in, I pass it on to my client. The additional benefit for me is that I tag those videos with my information as well as my client's information. When someone does a Google search for the client, our GHO pops up as well. That makes the GHO a mutually beneficial marketing tool! I have recorded some GHOs that became the number one search result for a client. *Oh . . .* and it's all *free*.

If you'd like to try out the CRM system, visit EasyFollowUpTool.com and check out Mothernode. For $60 a month, I now have a lead attraction tool that keeps track of all the leads that I help my clients acquire. The benefit of using Mothernode is that after someone fills out the form, they are immediately directed to the website of your choice. Generally, I send someone to my Facebook page to keep them engaged with OurMarketingGuy.com.

Please note: Google changes the process of Google Hang Outs quite often as they refine and improve it so some of this information may go out of date.

I am using GHOs to market our company.
◯ YES ◯ NO

"With Google I'm starting to burn out
on knowing the answer to everything.
People in the year 2020 are going to be nostalgic
for the sensation of feeling clueless."
Douglas Coupland

28

No Website? Are You Kidding Me?

As I was writing this book, I came across a flyer for Promotionally Minded, which announced moving our offices in 1998. Part of that flyer told our clients to look for our new website. What is amazing is *not* that in 1998 it was still unusual for companies to have a website, but in *this* century some business people that I speak with do not see the need for one. If you are reading this book, though, I would bet you are not one of those soon-not-to-be-in-business entrepreneurs.

Your website is one of the most important parts of your business. Years ago, pre-web, you had to have an incredible brochure, mailer, and leave-behinds. Those are still useful and important, but now, prior to doing business with you, people can, and will, check you out on the Internet. Their first stop will be to look for your website. It is the starting point for where you do business. Your website *is* your new brochure and it can do a lot more than ink on paper. It's often going to be the first impression people have of you and your business so make sure it's a good one!

So here are a few things to make sure you include on your website.

A blog: organic SEO (we'll be talking about SEO later) is improved when your website is constantly updated. By blogging regularly (daily, weekly) you will be found more efficiently.

A way to build your prospect list—this can be in the form of a free report, or get our newsletter—but the better the lead magnet, the more effective your list-building efforts.

A way to build your client list: by offering that same report for a small dollar amount ($3.97 to $9.97) you can create a list of customers that you can further prospect to. If they spend money, they are more apt to actually *read* what they buy from you and like what you are offering them. When teaching a marketing seminar, I often ask how many people have downloaded a free report and never even read it. The percentage is always quite high. By using this "tripwire" we can create more sales. There is a lot more to the concept of tripwire sales on the Internet, but that is for another book.

Video: the more video the better. It increases organic SEO because it is more difficult than simply writing words. Video can be a welcome on your front page, a short video for each of your services, included on your blog (shoot your blog as a video, then transcribe it as the written half), and a way to include *lots* of testimonials.

When we are designing websites for our clients, I am frequently asked how long a website will last. I am also frequently told that "I created a website, six years ago in a three-hour class." The short answer is three to four years and it should be updated constantly.

Important note: We just had a discussion about your website, you can ditto all of this to have a mobile app (short for application) for your company. More and more Internet traffic is being done on smartphones so in addition to making your website responsive to being seen on portable devices, you should also consider having an application created. This is something that your web person should be able to do, but if not, they are not very expensive to create. If you need help finding someone awesome, contact us.

We have a world class website and are developing our organic SEO.
◯ YES ◯ NO

"As useful as websites and journals are, there's real value in books, too."
Jamais Cascio

29

Building Your Website the Right Way

We have all heard the phrase "too good to be true." When it comes to websites, please understand that there are no shortcuts with search engine optimization and many other Internet marketing tools. Companies offering free website construction have to make up their costs somehow. Many of them recover their costs with web hosting and if you cancel, you lose your website *and* your URL because they have registered it in their name. Their sites are also set up with internal code that promotes their site as much as it does yours. They even drop their website URLs on the bottom page of your site, something which has been out of favor for years now. Unless, of course, they are willing to pay you a monthly fee.

So what do you do? For one thing, ignore the ads that say you can do it yourself for free.

Next, look around for websites that do what you want yours to do. Call those companies and get referrals. And when you call those web designers, ask for five referrals of sites they have built. After they give them to you, ask for the *next* five. I want you to use developers with *lots* of incredible experience under their belts.

As of the printing of this book, you should have your site built in WordPress. It is the program that is being favored by all the major search engines. It is open source code which allows a lot of developers to put in their own improvements. Kind of like jazz musicians can all get the same sheet music but play the pieces in a slightly different way.

Your developer should include a few hours of update time in their price, because you will want a few changes, and they should show you how to add new blog posts.

I also suggest that you go to YouTube and watch several videos on how to add a blog post to your site. You have to know how to add video, web forms, links to other sites, and photos. You also have to know how to add tags to your blog so that the search engines know how to deliver eyeballs to what you write.

Very, very important: The headers on your website should *not* read like 80% of websites do—"Promotionally Minded/contact" or "Promotionally

52

Minded/About Us." Those should be keywords: "Marketing Plans by Promotionally Minded" or "How To Create Marketing Plans by Our Marketing Guy". No one searches for "dentist contact us." They search "dentist Los Angeles" or "Miami personal injury attorney." Or "how do I find a good contractor." Get my point? We need to have lots of prime key words so people know how to find you.

There is a lot more that goes into it, but these basics will get you ahead of most of your competitors.

I am ahead of the game by using key word headers.
○ YES   ○ NO

"On the Internet, news is consumed a la carte.
If someone shows up on the main page of a website
and doesn't see anything of interest, they leave.
This negatively impacts ad revenues.
The solution on the Internet is to pack news websites
full of things that will draw people in,
regardless of whether they are news or not."
Drew Curtis

30

What Is in a Name?

While we are talking about websites, let's chat about what to call it. Here are some ideas.

Your company name is a no-brainer because it is your brand.

Your personal name is also a no-brainer because you are also the brand. If you have a common name, add your middle name or initial. Regardless of which URL you use, you should definitely reserve your name. If you have a common name and it is taken, add your middle initial.

There is nothing wrong with amusing and memorable URLs. We own OurMarketingGuy.com for our brand, but we also own OMGMarketingPlans.com, OurMarketingChecklist.com, BrandCamp101.com, and for those who are a bit more laid back, OurMarketingDude.com. We own our corporate name, PromotionallyMinded.com, but so many people make the mistake of calling us Professionally Minded, that we bought that one, too. You can use a 301-redirect and have more than one name point to the same site.

When creating the names, remember that the longer the URL, the more chances someone will mistype it. If your name is too long, have a descriptive URL instead. For example, one of the services our company promotes is a client-contact system called SendOutCards. My assigned URL for that is www.SendOutCards.com/26543. I chose to use something easier to use and remember: www.IDeserveItAll.com, *and* www.GodIHateMyBoss.com.

You must own these URL names. Do not allow your web person to buy the domain for you and keep it in their account. If they are going to register it for you, make sure they make you the registrant and the administrator. There are countless stories of companies who hire a snake-oil web designer who not only does a bad job, but hijacks your name. So let me ask you, the Internet is real estate. Do you want to own or rent?

You should have your website built on your own URL hosting account. If you use one of the many services that offer to host it for free and build it for free, you are going to get exactly the value you paid for. These sites use all the SEO "juice" to market themselves, not you.

**We are using the best and most memorable URLS
to promote our company.**

◯ YES   ◯ NO

---

*"What's in a name? That which we call a rose
by any other name would smell as sweet."*
William Shakespeare

31

Twenty-seventh Floor, Please

Your elevator pitch must nail it. This is like vaulting in the Olympics—there is the run up, the jump, the mid-air twist, and you have to stick the landing. It should last about the same amount of time, too.

There are several ways of doing a pitch.

One way that I am borrowing and adapting from a friend works like this: When most people are asked what they do, they answer with their occupation—I'm a stockbroker, I'm a realtor, I'm an ornithologist. When you respond that way people picture you selling stocks which they already have or cannot afford, putting a sign in front of their house when they are not ready to move, or sitting below a tree with a pair of binoculars.

Instead, begin with something that will attract attention and make the person asking the question pay closer attention. In this example you could tell the asker that you "make American industry hum." You could also say, "you're the reason people retire early." If you are a realtor, you could say, "you're in charge of short-term signage. You put them up and take them down sixty days later." You could also say, you're "in charge of putting kids in pools." As for the last one, try saying "You know how some people say they're for the birds? Well I am!"

The basic formula for this is "You know how _____? Well I _____."

Here are more examples: "You know how most people are so busy learning how to do what they do that they don't learn how to market what they do? Well I'm the one who fills in those blanks and increases sales." Or, "You know how some people know that social media exists but don't do much with it for business? Well we show companies how to use it to *increase* business." Or, "You know how some people have a website, but don't see how it generates much money? Well, we turn them into cash machines."

Say, "You know how _____," and then you bring up a situation that your clients face.

Say, "Well my company _____," and then you describe how you solve it.

Sometimes, your elevator speech will just hit you by accident. One day, I just happened to blurt out "At Promotionally Minded, we pollute the world one t-shirt, calendar, and coffee mug at a time." Laughter followed. And I was insta-pissed. That was *not* supposed to be the elevator speech, but people *got* it. Immediately. And they laughed. And in future years, they all remember it. And they call us for promotional products.

Remember . . . sometimes it is better to be lucky than good.

I have a locked-in elevator speech.
◯ YES   ◯ NO

---

*"Life is like an elevator: on your way up, sometimes,
you have to stop and let some people off."*
Hank Yuloff

"If you die in an elevator, be sure to push the 'up' button.
Sam Levenson

32

Tiger Practices, and We Can All Take a Lesson

It was the Saturday morning of the 2014 Masters. I was working in my office, and watching the professional golfers warm up. I am *not* a golfer. I have played, but am not an expert. But I do love watching the Masters. Call me odd, but let's get to the point of this tip.

As I was watching the players on the practice green (yes, I was watching them *practice*) the commentators mentioned a putting drill that Tiger Woods does every day; he lines up two golf tees about eight inches apart, puts a ball between them, and uses the tees to get used to putting the exact same way every time. They then said a couple of other players watched Tiger and started doing the exact same thing. The comment was, "Do you think it's the first time someone has mimicked the #1 golfer in the world?" The other commentator answered, "And I bet that it is going to be copied all around the country now."

And it makes sense.

Why *wouldn't* we practice what we do? Why should we be complacent and satisfied with how we do our job? It is why I took dozens of hours of continuing education in the promotional products industry and qualified for my Certified Advertising Specialist (CAS) designation. And even though I am a pretty good graphic artist, I am always looking to learn new tricks that I can add to my tool bag.

In addition to teaching workshops on marketing, I attend lots of seminars ,which allow me to practice *my* craft. I want to make every swing of my marketing clubs count.

So when Tiger gets out his two golf tees, and starts dropping six golf balls, going through the same practice routine, it makes logical sense for all of us, whether we play golf or not, to take a lesson from a master, *at* the Masters, and get better focused on our own skills.

I practice my skills and hone my craft.
○ YES ○ NO

"I'm aware if I'm playing at my best I'm tough to beat. And I enjoy that."
Tiger Woods

33

Research, Research, Research

You should make it a point to know your competition, and determine what it will take for you to win business from them. Knowing their target markets helps you either create a better message or change your own targets to increase your sales. Here are a couple of examples.

If you are in the building trade, what hours does your biggest competitor *really* work? What do they charge? Is their radio ad a big come-on? Do they specialize in single-family dwellings or commercial buildings? Do they do new construction or do they do remodel and. repair?

When I was in college the biggest competitor to our student newspaper was a weekly shopper. Each Thursday, our reps would pour through the shopper, looking for new advertisers we could cold call. If they wanted to target the college market, our publication was better suited for their needs because we were on campus and it was picked up daily by their potential customers. Also, our prices were better for a more highly-targeted product.

Other ways of researching your industry are to check out the websites for competitors who are nowhere near you geographically. If you are in Los Angeles, check out Miami, New Orleans, Charlotte, and Chicago. Never ever copy those sites, just do a "drive-by" to see what kinds of offers they have, the way they blog, and how they do what they do.

I keep track of my competition.
◯ YES   ◯ NO

"If we knew what it was we were doing,
it would not be called research, would it?"
Albert Einstein

"Money won't buy happiness, but it will pay the
salaries of a large research staff to study the problem."
Bill Vaughan

34

Being Unique Is a Common Proposition

No marketing tips book would be complete without discussing unique selling propositions (USP). You have probably heard the words unique selling proposition—it is a very common phrase that all consultants and guru-wannabes toss out. But what is your value proposition? What makes your business unique?

It is the way you sell yourself in a way that is different from your competitors. It allows your customers to relate to you in a way that is, well, so unique that it makes them want to be a part of what it is that you do. It is what makes you memorable while proving you are the best.

So let's try and put one together for you.

It's a lot more than a famous slogan such as:

- "It's the real thing" for Coca Cola.
- "We try harder" for Avis.
- "The ultimate driving machine" for BMW.
- "What happens in vegas . . ." for that little city in Nevada.
- "We pollute the world, one t-shirt, calendar, and coffee mug at a time" for Promotionally Minded (just seeing if you were paying attention).

It has to tell your clients—and probably your competitors if they are paying attention— what you and your company do that the typical prospect may not have any idea about. You're probably not going to be lucky enough to come up with M&Ms and their melting in the mouth, not in the hand; but if you work hard, you will come up with one.

We have an accountant client that has worked with dozens of start-up companies. He and his partner are experts in assisting them with developing financing and getting off the ground. They have found that it is one of the best ways for them to acquire and keep business, and most of their competitors do not want the challenge of working with new companies because of the chance that a new company will not succeed.

My USP? Thanks for asking: We are looking for business people who know they are the best at what they do but want to defeat a competitor who is outspending them. Our job is to target their demographic markets to out-perform that free-spending competitor.

Here is another way of describing this chapter. When you are in a group meeting, watch how many people, when describing their business, say they give good service. Have you met anyone that would not say they do? That is not a USP. Saying you give the kind of service they always wanted and describing exactly how you are different, is much closer.

I can describe my company USP easily and succinctly.
○ YES ○ NO

"Feeling unique is no indication of uniqueness."
Douglas Coupland

"Discover your uniqueness. Learn to exploit it in the service of others, and you are guaranteed success, happiness, and prosperity."
Larry Winget

35

Speaking of Advertising Slogans

For an idea to stick it has to change behavior. All of our companies are trying to change the behaviors of people who do business with us. One of the ways we do it is to advertise and to share a message which resonates with our audience.

Here are some of the best ever. Notice what they say about their products while creating an image in your head.

Snap, Crackle, Pop

He Keeps Going, and Going, and Going . . .

We make money the old-fashioned way. We earn it.

Nothing Runs Like a Deere

Be All You Can Be

Notice, not *one* of them says they give great service, or have the lowest prices. By a show of hands, how many of you out there reading this book give crappy service and are more expensive than you deserve to be?

Amusing, witty, thought-evoking, mental-picture drawing, and not too long!

My advertising slogan is :

_____

_____

_____

_____

_____

_____

"Many a small thing has been made large by the right kind of advertising."
Mark Twain

"Advertising is the art of convincing people to spend money they don't have for something they don't need."
Will Rogers

"Advertising is salesmanship mass produced.
No one would bother to use advertising
if he could talk to all his prospects face-to-face. But he can't."
Morris Hite

36

Gooooal!

Raise one finger for each time you have heard someone tell you to set goals, have a plan, and work it and blah blah blah. Oh well, heck, you know, you really should set goals for each separate project.

Prior to the project being finished, set some specific targets for a soft launch, and a hard launch. As the project is launched, plan on what you expect after thirty days, sixty days, ninety days, and then quarterly thereafter. Do not be afraid to make adjustments along the way.

We planned a new website for OurMarketingGuy.com. For that site we made several goals and missed *every* one of them. But it did give us a target. We were constantly on top of what we were doing and it helped us lock down all the different parts of it. This book was charted out on a wipe and write board. The number of marketing tips, how long I was going to give myself to go through notes taken at seminars, my blog, and sales presentations that I have made.

One of the most important parts of goal setting is to make them time specific. Choose a date that is definitely acheivable with a bit of effort.

It makes a lot of sense to use a blank calendar, and write the delivery date on it. From there, work backwards for each part of the product until you hit the current date or the start date, whichever is later. For example, if you need sixty days to write a book on marketing tips, and you want it finished by the end of March, then you should start at the beginning of the year (preferably in Sedona, Arizona near a vortex).

I have my time-specific goals written down, and here are three of them.
○ YES   ○ NO

1. _____

_____

2. _____

_____

3. _____

_____

_____

"The greater danger for most of us lies not in setting our aim too high and falling short, but in setting our aim too low and achieving our mark."
Michaelangelo

"A goal is a dream with a deadline."
Napoleon Hill

"Hokey smokes, this planning stuff is hard."
Hank Yuloff

"The fact is, we don't manage time, we manage ourselves within chunks of time."
Joe Buzzello

*"If you're not stubborn, you'll give up on experiments too soon.
And if you're not flexible, you'll pound your head against the wall
and you won't see a different solution to a problem you're trying to solve."*
Jeff Bezos

37

Crisis PR Is Not the Best
Public Relations Strategy

Very early on January 9, 2014 the city of Charleston and 300,000 of its residents were left without tap water because of a chemical spill into the Elk River. Depending upon your political bent, there are different people to blame, ranging from "no one, stuff goes on, stop crying about it," to "the company is at fault," to "the government blew it at every level." We don't need to participate in the debate, we want to discuss what happens when your company is the lead story on CNN every hour for days, or your local television station, or your local paper.

The company that owned the tank farm that experienced the leak is Freedom Industries. At first report by the Associated Press, they did not seem to be out of compliance with West Virginia laws, but their tanks were last inspected in 1991. So where did it go wrong? And how could your company be splashed all over CNN if your company does nothing that deals with anything remotely dangerous?

Whether or not you have a company with potential for environmental damage or, for example, you are a psychiatrist whose patient does something horrific, or you have a delivery truck that hired a driver who's foot simply slipped off the brake and drove through a mini-mall and ruined twelve cars, or you have hired an employee and could not possibly know everything that happened in his or her past, you need to be prepared.

Start to think of all the things that could go wrong with your company. If you sell a product, what are all the possible negatives? Could food go bad? Could someone swallow small parts of it? When people come to our promotional product company, Promotionally Minded, and ask for certain products, we make sure to go through some of the possible negatives. At the extreme, imprinted condoms bring with them certain amusement, but could also get you blamed for unwanted pregnancies. Yes, some of these things could take you *way* out to the extreme, but you need to make that long list.

The next step is to begin to discuss what you could do to mitigate and solve the problems. If X happens, then Y is what we will do. Some companies even have important paragraphs about their company and their positive involvement in the community ready to be inserted into a press release.

And how *will* you tell your story? At the Encino Chamber of Commerce, we have a policy that if anyone asks a board member for the chamber's opinion on a matter, our *only* answer is to refer them to the CEO of the organization. One voice, one face. Centralized information dissemination is vital. The president or owner of the company, even a small company, may not be the right person. If the chamber did not have someone who was good in front of a reporter, as has been the case in the past, that should not be the face with our message. If you are a sole proprietor, it could be a wise move to have a public relations or marketing firm on a small retainer for just such an emergency, and to help you go through this exercise. In the Freedom Industries case, they taped a phone number to their signs and asked people to dial the crisis PR firm that they hired (and who dropped them two days later).

The president of Freedom Industries, Gary Southern, went out to talk to reporters with a bottle of water in his hands and drank from it while asking questions; that made for a bad image. He also did not answer all of the questions. He was seen as evasive. He was under a lot of stress, and probably just wanted to get through the press conference. But a repentant company goes a long way towards solving some legal problems down the road. It does not get you off the hook legally, but transparency makes for a kinder jury pool and fosters forgiveness.

Your website and social media will be very important in a crisis. Make sure that the people who have the keys to publish them are aware that there is an emergency plan, and that they are not to take things into their own hands, even if they just want to help. I am one of the administrators of my chamber Facebook page, but I would never post anything in a crisis situation without discussing the posts with the CEO, president, and our legal team. It's part of my expertise, and I know the rules. It's on of the reasons that I *am* an administrator. To the credit of Freedom Industries, they left their website alone, although if they had a blog page, they could be talking about the steps they were taking to work with the community.

Part of your plan should be following the rules for your industry. There are indications that Freedom Industries did not respond appropriately. A state law required the immediate reporting of leaks from chemical tanks, but it was reported that environmental clean-up workers were on the spill site at 11:15 a.m. Thursday, January 9, 2014 because of a call from the water company —not from Freedom Industries. Stay out in front of *any* challenges. It is the only way your story can be told.

Make sure that your plan with all its contingencies lives in a binder as well as on a hard drive. No power means no plan and in a crisis, you do not want to be guessing. You may want to keep a copy of this binder in a remote location, as well.

The reason we talk about remote locations is important. When Sony Pictures' network was hacked by North Korea at the end of 2014, they were left with their staff having to work weeks to recreate terabytes of information. Their crisis public relations plan could have planned for the basics, but they had to react to fill in the blanks regarding the release of The Interview. These details were worked on by Legal Affairs, Marketing, Accounting, and Information Technology. The decisions they had to make were how to release the film, and how to replace the information which was stolen.

Of course, Sony would have had a difficult time pre-planning for an international incident that forced them to reconsider the release date and change their method of distribution, but there are lots of things that they *could* envision—like earthquakes, a star dying just prior to release, or the chairman being found in bed in a scandalous situation. Having remote back ups for any size company makes these decisions easier and more quickly made.

**I have looked at my business from a "what if" point of view
and I have a plan prepared.**
○ YES   ○ NO

*"We learn something every day, and lots of times
it's that what we learned the day before was wrong."*
Bill Vaughan

38

You Are the Fairest of Them All

The magic mirror on the wall is supposed to tell us that the look of our company is the fairest of them all. But is it? You should develop a great look and feel to everything you do and make sure it is *consistent*. You need a logo or icon to make it easier for your target to instantly recognize you.

Unless you have a degree in design, you're not a designer. Farm that stuff out to someone who has experience in this field. It is an investment that will pay back. Double ditto for writers. You need a strong corporate and branding voice. Not everyone can do this. Find someone who can, then pay them ridiculous amounts to do it.

I constantly have to remind myself of this for my own marketing. I regularly design the look and the voice for my clients, but when it is for myself, I realize that the same blinders that apply to my clients affect me as well.

My first book is called *49 Stupid Things People Do with Their Business Cards . . . and How To Fix Them.* Having years of experience in design, I thought I would take a shot at doing something I had only done once before—put together a cover for the book. Thankfully I have some friends who were brutally honest with me and I hired an artist with *tons* of experience in that area. The cover was awesome—and you can see it for yourself at www.49StupidThings.com I even have the covers which were rejected there (marketing tip—that was a shameless plug. Shameless plugs, when they give value, are a good thing).

In retrospect, I think that I blew it because I attempted to make the book cover tie in to my Our Marketing Guy brand. That was a mistake, because though I was the author of the book and the person behind the OMG brand, the two projects are not under the same marketing umbrella.

There are several websites that offer very inexpensive ways to get this sort of thing done. I am not in favor of using them because you should have a strong, continuing relationship with your design team and paying $20 for a logo is not going to generate the best representation for your brand.

My company has a consistent image and it is amazing.
◯ YES ◯ NO

"Don't be afraid to give up the good to go for the great."
John D. Rockefeller

*"The reciprocal nature of networking establishes a relationship
instead of a one-night-stand."*
Dan Schawbel

39

Business Cards, Seven Simple Square Inches of Recognition

As long as we are discussing your look, and my book—*49 Stupid Things People Do with Business Cards . . . and How To Fix Them*—let's talk about your business cards. It used to be as simple as a name. The practice of carrying a calling card was first used in France during the time of Louis XIV. Not to be undone, the members of high society in England used them to announce their arrivals at a home as well. In fact, without them, a gentleman was not allowed into the household.

As things often go, once one niche group discovers something useful, it becomes more common in use. But instead of social arrivals, business cards were for the first time used to promote tradesmen. More like flyers than cards, they were posted to advertise a merchant's location. Very useful in times before street names and numbers.

Time passed, and using a card to make one's social presence known faded while the use of trade cards or business cards has flourished, most often becoming one of the first things a business purchases.

The information on a card expanded from company name, logo, and location to include the proprietor's name, title, and address. A short while after Alexander Graham Bell's invention, we added phone numbers, then toll-free numbers, then fax numbers, and finally cell phone numbers. And in the last decade we have all added web addresses and email addresses. A good business card should also say what you *do*!

Business cards are going to be one of the least expensive marketing tools you have and they should be with you all the time. I always keep an extra box in my car.

A couple of very important things: Do *not* use those cheap online-only services. They are upselling you on lots of things you do not need and you are forced to share the same design as thousands of other business owners. *Also*, it is okay to have two or three different business cards that are targeted to different markets.

Do you need all of this? In a word, *yes*. Your business card is an introduction to your company and to what you do. Its job is to make it as easy as possible for someone to contact you. But remember they want to contact you on *their* terms. So if you do not include your email, you may not ever hear from a Gen X or Gen Y'er. No address? Then Baby Boomers will not believe you are a legitimate business. They also won't know where to send your check. And after all, that *is* why we are in business—the check!

My business card would not qualify
to be in Hank Yuloff's business card book.
◯ YES   ◯ NO

(If you are not sure, send a jpg to WeLove@OurMarketingGuy.com and we will look at it for you.)

"Our business in life is not to get ahead of others, but to get ahead of ourselves –
to break our own records, to outstrip our yesterday by our today"
Stewart B. Johnson

"When the first impression is partially determined by your business card
why the heck would you not make it as professional as possible?"
Hank Yuloff

40

Old School, New School Communication

In the 21st Century, there is an increased tidal wave of Internet-based ways to communicate with our clients and prospects. While many of these methods are incredible, there also is a need to be disconnected from it all.

When reaching out to your public, don't just rely on e-mail and texts. The reason for overload is obvious, but when you have someone like me with several e-mail addresses for various businesses, you may be inadvertently overlooked.

Make sure to incorporate old-school approaches as well: personal cards, thank-you notes, and face-to-face meetings are still important to create stronger relationships. You can even (gasp) pick up the phone and call them.

Many of my most Internet-connected friends brag on social media sites about the meetings they just had with new decision makers. That seems to be where they are closing the deal.

**Our company is connected to our target audience
in more than one way.**
◯ YES ◯ NO

---

*"Never overlook the power of nuanced communication.
But to embrace the power, we have to look it right in the face."*
Hank Yuloff

41

Same Time, Same Place, Same Marketing

When we took a work-cation to Sedona, we had to rent a car. The one I got, had roll up windows. *Roll Ups*! I had not had a car with that incredible technology for a couple of decades. It made me think about how accustomed to power windows I have become. If I want a window open, I simply hit a button. Suddenly there was no button to push. And that made me think of how often we get used to doing the same things with our marketing (it is *not* a reach—work with me here).

One of the cardinal rules of advertising is that repetition is important. I try and tell myself that when I hear the same ads on my favorite radio station for the 100th time. Or, when I see the same flyers in my mailbox. Or, when the television airwaves are populated with the same television ads, over and over and over.

If it's that cute kid promoting the online investment house it's one thing, but that guy who hawks freeeeee mattresses is annoying as heck. Maybe if I was not constantly tuned in I would not hear and see them all the time, but I believe there is a certain point at which an ad or series of ads has diminishing returns.

Picture a bell curve. We start on the left hand side, and move our way up the curve. At some point on the way up, we really hear the ad. We then hear it several times while we make a decision to seek more information, either on the Internet, on the phone, or in person. Then we get to the top of that peak of the bell curve and begin to head down the other side. It is somewhere on that right side of the peak that the ad loses effectiveness. We have watched it, sought information, and then made a decision.

Product life cycle: The key in advertising campaigns using *any media* is to keep track of how it is working and have the next campaign ready to go when you recognize that the previous one has peaked and is heading downhill. Planning the next one is a constant effort.

Keeping it fresh can be as simple as changing the message that you use within the regular methods of advertising. It can also be an opportunity to try the same message within some other form of delivery system. For example, if you are doing radio ads, try the same message on television. Or if you are sending ads through e-mail, you may want to try it as a direct mail piece. Another way of trying to check the return on investment of your message is to try a different message within the same method of advertisement delivery. This is called segmentation.

We keep our marketing ads and messages fresh and ever changing.
◯ YES   ◯ NO

"Your premium brand had better be delivering something special, or it's not going to get the business."
Warren Buffett

42

Branding Is a Part of the Marketing Process

Branding. Seems to be a one-word catch phrase that is all over the place, huh? Just as the phrases "new paradigm" and "out of the box" have been. But if you look at the word as a reminder, it helps you get focused on your message.

So what *is* branding? I recently interviewed a brand strategist and her definition of branding is that it is a feeling or an emotion that is tied to you and your product or service, "It is your logo and everything that logo represents."

The goal in our branding is to create a positive emotion so that when we put together your marketing plan, we are promoting an already positive feeling.

For small companies, the personality of the owner is going to permeate the brand. I will say here what I tell my solo-preneur clients: The name of your company is important and the logo of your company is important, but *you* are the brand.

As you hire more people, they will begin to blend into your company's personality but it is important that you remember to keep a firm watch on what is said to clients, how it is said, and how clients and employees interact.

My favorite example is when you walk down the aisle at a grocery store and are looking for a cola product, more than 90% of us are looking for Coca Cola or Pepsi. We are not searching for the product, we are searching for the logo. We are not reading labels, we are scanning logos.

According to the brand strategist that I interviewed, when you are putting together the logo, you should keep in mind that something abstract and simple will allow you to build meaning into it in terms of reinforcing the messaging. So using a rainbow or a flower is not necessarily a good choice because people already have an image in their head as to what those things mean to them. "What happens when you do that, use those symbols, is that you end up looking like everyone else," she says.

Boiled down: By deciding on what the philosophy is behind what you do, before creating your marketing plan, when you put your message together in the sales and marketing process, you will be able to be clearer and your messages will stand out.

I can visualize my brand.
○ YES   ○ NO

And it is:

_____

_____

_____

_____

_____

_____

_____

_____

"A brand for a company is like a reputation for a person.
You earn reputation by trying to do hard things well."
Jeff Bezos

43

Video Is Very Important to Your Marketing

When Our Marketing Guy puts together marketing plans for clients, we tell them they have to start blogging, and they get a little tense. Then we tell them they have to add *video* to their blogs and they get *very* tense.

I totally understand why, because their first thought is, "I don't like how I look on video." Yes, *you* are not the only one who thinks that way. But look at *me*! One quick look at my photo and you can see that I get it. But the thing is, once we get those new clients, we are going to have to see them at one time or another, in person or through Google Hangouts so they are going to know what we look like. It's time for us all to grow up and get over it. Or I can put a photo of George Clooney in front of my video cam.

The reason we are doing video is that it will get you more "points" from search engines. That nebulous thing called *search engine optimization,* which brings more people to your blog and your website, is increased by using video. You get more "credit" because search engines know that adding video to your blog is harder to do than just typing your 300-500 word blog and hitting *enter.* You have to shoot it, in some cases edit it, upload it, properly tag it, and then drop the embed code into the right place in your WordPress blog. In some cases, you will want to *re*-shoot it. The video attached to one of my blogs was shot many times. Either I tripped over the words, or a phone rang (tip: turn off your phone when you shoot your blog), or there was some other outside noise interruption. I give you permission not to go with the first take. Just remember you are getting extra points for shooting video. It's like doing a book report on a sick day in school!

There are lots of places to get tips on shooting great videos, but here are five tips to make your videos better:

1. Keep your background simple. Plants against a blank wall are good.

2. Using notes is okay! Go back and look at my videos (*please*). I hold a note sheet *all* the time. It helps me put in all my points, and it adds a human quality to your video.

3. I love shooting outside, it adds more interest to the video, but if you do not have a clip on microphone, you are going to get wind noise and that *sucks*! Nothing worse than shooting your video blog in one perfect take only to hear that it was ruined by wind.

4. Have someone you trust shoot your videos. Give them permission to tell you that *that* take was not your best. Believe them and do not get mad at them for telling you the truth.

5. Keep your blog videos under two minutes long. When people decide to watch a video, they *always* look at the length of the video to decide if they are willing to give you their attention. My target is even less— one minute to a minute and a half.

6. You should upload the videos to your YouTube channel, but please keep a copy of every video on your hard drive in case something happens to your YouTube account.

I use video to market my business and it is amazing.
◯ YES   ◯ NO

"If one does not know to which port one is sailing, no wind is favorable."
Lucius Annaeus Seneca

*"If you listen to your fears, you will die
never knowing what a great person you might have been."*
Robert H. Schuller

*"Just because something doesn't do what you planned it to do
doesn't mean it's useless."*
Thomas A. Edison

44

E-mail, G-mail, Got Change for a Marketing Dollar?

My first e-mail address (still have it!) was a Yahoo address. I noticed early on that they had a *spam* folder where lots of mass mailing e-mails ended up. Cool! About half of the direct mail I get, I did not need to open most of the time anyway. In those days, e-mail open rates were about 60% which *far* exceeded direct mail, and it was free.

Fast forward a number of years and bulk e-mail rates have plummeted. Most marketers have not gotten the idea that just because it is free does not mean you can just keep sending message after message after message to your target market. Especially when you make that target a lot larger because since mailing is free, you might as well mail to a million when you really only want to target 100,000. Free made it the favorite of marketers everywhere. When we put together marketing plans at Our Marketing Guy we sometimes have to overcome this belief that free equals better. Free is good, but not the only way to market.

Fast forward to today and Google has changed its G-mail inbox to split out e-mails by types and there are lots of direct marketers who are *freaking out.*

This is a partial e-mail that I got from one of them: "G-mail made a big change this week and whether you're a fan of the change or not, it *matters.* Why? Because e-mail is your (and my) #1 way of staying connected with each other, delivering your programs and attracting new clients. Think about it: *all* the free articles and training videos you get from me—gone. Even details about programs you've already paid for would be missed. Yikes!"

Well, they were not really gone—just segmented into the promotions area of your inbox. Clearly labeled and waiting for you. There is also a social media tab where your posting notifications will reside.

If you don't want to use these options, here are two ways to change them:

1. Click on the "Promotions" tab folder and find the e-mails of the newsletters you get all the time in there. Drag it to the "Primary" tab folder. A question will pop up and ask if you want to do this for future messages or e-mails from that person, Click "yes." Check your

"Promotions" inbox over the next few weeks to make sure nothing that you want to see is getting caught up here (this could include announcements for programs that you're already in).

2. *Turn off the new tab feature completely.* This is my favorite so you do not have to worry about e-mails being filtered by G-mail. Click on the "Setting" icon in the upper right hand corner of your screen and select "Settings" from the drop down menu. Click on the "Inbox" tab and unselect all categories except "Primary." Click the "Save Changes" button at the bottom of the screen.

It is perfectly alright to continue to use e-mail as a major marketing tool, if it is not your only tool. You have to know that the Internet is changing. At some point in the near future, e-mails are not going to be free and you better be prepared for that. You should use regular, terrestrial marketing tools if you want to stay on top.

As with all things Google, their e-mail system may change, so as it is updated, please accept my apologies.

I am building my client list with both e-mail addresses and physical addresses.
◯ YES   ◯ NO

"There is only one boss. The customer. And he can fire everybody in the company from the chairman on down, simply by spending his money somewhere else."
Sam Walton

"Effort only fully releases its reward after a person refuses to quit."
Napoleon Hill

"Hell, there are no rules here—we're trying to accomplish something."
Thomas A. Edison

45

Ten plus One Great Ways
(and Four Bad Ones) To Use QR Codes

When I look at magazines from the 1980s it becomes obvious that toll-free numbers were a popular tool to increase the response rates. "Call Toll-free for more information" was an advertiser's way of saying we are so confident in our product that we are willing to pick up the cost of your call. OurMarketingGuy.com has a toll free number by the way—(800)705-HANK (4265).

In the 1990s, the next step in providing easy contact was to begin adding website URLs to your ads. Next time you are at your dentist, take a look at the magazines in the waiting room and you will see that it still took a while to get those web addresses into the ads but now it is the rare exception that does *not* have a web address.

During the 1990s, QR codes (quick response codes) were developed as a way to quickly and directly bring someone to a specific place on the Internet via smartphones. These codes make it possible for a QR scanner application on your phone to deliver rich information via an image, just as a bar code does for a product. For more information on QR codes, you can go to our www.QRCroi.com website. For now, here are eleven good uses for you to use them:

1. Bring your target audiences a video message that goes along with your static one. Imagine a poster-sized ad for a show in a Las Vegas casino posted just outside the luggage area in the airport. With a snapshot it could help you purchase tickets for the show before you even catch a cab to your hotel.

2. Especially good on direct-mail pieces.

3. Promotionally Minded and Our Marketing Guy used a QR code to bring people to one of our marketing shows. It took people to a video we made with some of our presenters that gives free marketing tips.

4. Real estate agents can put QR codes on their For Sale signs outside a house so people can get a visual of the house before they even walk in.

5. I have seen them used at home improvement stores to give shoppers more information on plants they want to buy by linking each plant to an informational video.

6. Along those lines, a grocery store could bring shoppers to a recipe website with a QR code next to each product on their shelves.

7. On tradeshow badges—scan the badge for instant business cards. At those same tradeshows, a QR code can give a quick video sampling of the speakers that they have the choice of listening to.

8. Posters outside a theater can take a ticket buyer to the movie preview (I call them warnings) or by playing the preview before entering, it can give them a way to easily purchase tickets.

9. The betrothed bride and groom can put a message in their invitation including the important information, and use another one for guests to easily RSVP.

10. You can add them to a t-shirt give away (Promotionally Minded is *great* at adding them to the shirt designs) so that information about your business is easily accessible. By the way, on the back of the shirt or the sleeve is the best place to put them. Make them large enough so the scanner does not have to severely violate the personal space of the wearer.

11. I use them on my business cards to help people engage with me on Facebook and capture tons of free marketing advice.

Here are some unfortunate uses of QR codes:

1. For goodness sake, do *not* put them up high above a street on a billboard. You may be liable for drivers who try to scan while they drive.

2. In an e-mail: You don't really want someone to scan their computer screen. They are already *on* the Internet, just add the link.

3. Places where there is no readily available signal: In an airline magazine or anywhere below the ground floor of a building.

4. In an area where they are too small to be easily read. I suggest 3/4" or larger on the printed page and 2" square on a t-shirt.

I know what QR codes are and how to use them.
◯ YES   ◯ NO

"Sometimes when you innovate, you make mistakes.
It is best to admit them quickly,
and get on with improving your other innovations."
Steve Jobs

46

Outsourcing Cold Calls?
Five Things (plus a Bonus) to Remember

One day I got a phone call—a cold call. Before you move on with your work, let me set the stage. I am on the board of an organization that holds a major fundraising event each year that I am intimately involved with so when I received this call, I was very interested in hearing what was said.

The gentleman on the other end of the line was a staffer for a company that is a sponsor of the event this year. The company had taken on the task of calling other members to get them involved as well. This is not an easy task for any organization no matter what the event.

As he rambled through a few comments that seemed to be what he was told by someone else to say (and who did not have all the details), I was a bit disheartened, because this is, in effect, *my* message, too.

I know a lot of business people who are involved with a number of organizations that have lots of events, so this chapter is for you. If you or someone under your direction are making these calls, here are some points you need to cover:

1. Tell them what to say but let *them* say it. If they are not used to being on the phone, give them a script. Have it written out in a conversational tone, not a formal style. It can even be written in their own voice if you do it correctly. Give them the bullet points and have them practice being on the phone. Record it. Then go back and transcribe it. Now they are reading in their voice, not your voice or the formal voice. Example: "Good morning, Mr. Yuloff. How are you this fine day? The purpose for this call is to educate you on the benefits of taking part in a *cool* organization's annual large fundraising event." As opposed to, "Hey, Mr. Yuloff, this is Chelsea from Promotionally Minded. I know that you don't know me, but our companies are both members of the *cool* organization and I was hoping to pass along some information about the upcoming event. Is that ok?"

2. Three benefits: The mind can grasp units of three very easily. If you tell them up front what it is that you are doing, sharing three benefits

for their company, they may want to find out what they will miss if they don't listen. Ask your past participants what was the best part of the event for them.

3. Show Respect: You cannot tell your whole story in the minute that Mr. Yuloff is going to give you. He has other stuff to do. You may want to use these calls as bird dogging. "Mr. Yuloff, I don't want to take much of your time, we just wanted to give you a couple of reasons that you may want to exhibit and to see if we need to have one of the chairpersons call you to answer questions that you might have. Is that ok?" You are showing respect; you will have *the chairperson* call and give them extra attention. Even if you are a chair making these calls, you can gather prospects for the *other* chairs to call back.

4. Practice before turning them loose. My caller was almost "out the door" before he mentioned, seemingly as an afterthought, that his company was a sponsor and that they were holding a job fair at the event for veterans and that they are subsidizing two hundred hours of their income. He did not ask me if I *knew* any veterans who might need assistance. Go through it with your callers. Mock calls seem most silly to inexperienced sales people. They are not used to asking for the sale, especially money. That is why you may want these calls to be appointment setters.

5. Have your goal clearly stated; add an incentive to it. "So come by, check it out" should *never* be used on a call. Yes, I heard that in the call. Twice. And it was my caller's closing argument. Tell your callers what you expect out of these calls. It should not be "Here is a list of two hundred members. Call them and find out if they want a booth at *cool organization event*." They probably see that two hundred number and freeze up. Have some prize for each appointment they set for you.

6. Bonus tip: Have a second script ready for voice mail. Have the biggest benefit right up front. Make it short. Ask them to take action.

I am comfortable making cold calls.
○ YES   ○ NO

"Nolan Ryan said 'Pitching is easy. Preparation is hard.'
This baseball truth is also true in the sales profession.
Selling is easy. Preparing to sell is hard work."
Barbara Gerahaughty

47

My Mother Still Exists (on Mailing Lists)

What do Equinox, Time Warner Cable, a Prudential real estate agent in San Diego, and Roy's Restaurant have in common? In the last week, they all sent marketing pieces to my Mom, who passed away twelve years ago, or to my Dad, who is either already one of their customers or he is completely out of their demographic target. When you look at Equinox ads, they are *not* targeting eighty-year olds. Not even close. Their slogan is "It's Not Fitness. It's Life." That is *not* what octogenarians are thinking.

As for our cable company, why are you trying to sell us products we already have? They are obviously, or maybe not so obviously, mining their own customer list for expanded business, so better list management is necessary.

As for the real estate agent, I give her some credit. Dad moved out of the area, but still owns a property in her area. I should call her and ask how she got the updated mailing address (and ask her if she realizes that my parents are . . . uh . . . no longer living in the same place. This is the kind of thing that can cost you business. Those nerves can be very raw when a loved one passes away. I use a greeting card system (you can try it for free at www.CardsBy-Hank.com), which allows me to set up birthday cards to be sent over a year in advance. I only set them up a month to six weeks in advance because of this very thing. The cards are just .62 ($1.08 with postage) and keep me in touch with my customers easily.

As for the restaurant, I wonder what mailing list they bought that had my mom listed using only her name, on a street and in a city where she never lived.

The message here is that when you buy mailing lists, you have to negotiate a lot of extra names to make up for the bad ones. If you create your own list organically from people you meet in the course of business, make sure you mail to it often enough to keep it up to date. When the "bad ones" come back invest the time to see what happened. It is the best way to not lose touch.

I have an up-to-date mailing list.
○ YES ○ NO

"The wrong person will never give you what you want, but they'll make sure they get what they want from you."
Sonya Parker

48

They Call Themselves Graphic Artists

Many people who call themselves graphic artists are . . . let's just say . . . lacking. They are the ones who fancy themselves *artists* first, the *graphics* part is just an inconvenient beginning of the phrase. Let me give you just the latest example. Our promotional product company, Promotionally Minded, was creating an order of logo-imprinted bags for a magazine and their artist could not send us vector artwork because: "When designing in Photoshop, you cannot create vector art. We created your logo in Photoshop for many reasons, which involves much more design capability other than just vector, such as blending it into photos on the cover of the magazine, etc. What I sent is high resolution and should suffice."

The short answer: It only suffices if the magazine does not care what their logo looks like.

The slightly longer answer: This artist does not have the ability to create vector artwork and is blowing smoke into our clients face. The first logo they sent was such a small file as to make me think that they right-clicked it off their website. Hey, it happens. The professionals will take the time to let you know the difference (because they *know* the difference) between rasterized (pixilated) artwork and vector artwork and how they are each used.

In order to make this crystal clear, a few definitions are in order:

Vector artwork: Vector-based graphics can be scaled using algorithms within the program that creates them—Adobe Illustrator or Corel Draw, for example. A piece of artwork, a logo or such, can be made larger or smaller, and it remains crystal clear. You do not need to modify the graphic when you want to change size.

Rasterized graphics: When artwork is created in a program that is based upon pixels, for example Photoshop, when it is enlarged, it gets "fuzzy." In printing, fuzzy is not good. Whenever you resize a pixelated image (and you only want to scale down or you get fuzzy), you must change the fixed size of the image.

Microsoft Word is a program designed to process text. It is not the best program to use in producing artwork, advertisements, logos or any other marketing tools.

So the point of this marketing tip is for me to give you a sense as to what *real* graphic artists are like. My biggest tip? If they can only design your logo in Photoshop—*run*. You found an "artist" but not someone who can create your company image and prepare if for all the different ways it needs to be used. A professional designer will have all the necessary tools (and skill) to prepare your artwork for any needed outcome. I am pretty good with graphics because I have to be. Logos and image are my life. But I also know when a project should be sent to a higher-level graphic artist. And by that, I do *not* mean to farm it out to some cheap Internet alternative. Think long term and develop a relationship with that graphic designer.

I have my logo available in every main format.
○ YES   ○ NO

**I promise to never just "right-click" the logo
off my website as a way of sharing it.**
○ YES   ○ NO

---

*"Every artist dips his brush in his own soul,
and paints his own nature into his pictures."*
Henry Ward Beecher

*"Creativity is allowing yourself to make mistakes.
Art is knowing which ones to keep."*
Scott Adams

"Painting is just another way of keeping a diary."
Pablo Picasso

49

Learn to Manage Color! RGB, CMYK, and Pantone, Oh My!

When it comes to printed materials, colors are often the most critical part. Getting the colors you see on screen to translate to a printed piece can be tricky. The key is knowing your color modes.

RGB color mode is used by devices like your computer monitor and TV to display color images. The RGB color model uses red, green, and blue light to create an array of colors. RGB is an additive color model, meaning as you add colors of light together you create other colors. People producing websites would use the RGB color mode to create their work since it will always be viewed on screen.

CMYK color mode is used in the print world. Specific ink colors, Cyan, Magenta, Yellow, and Black are mixed together to create an array of colors. The CMYK color model is a subtractive model where colors are created by mixing a limited set of inks together. By mixing a percentage of each ink together some wavelengths of light are being absorbed (subtracted). For example, pretend you are holding a printed flyer with a solid green background, the ink mixture used to create that green is absorbed into the paper and when light hits the surface of the flyer specific color wave lengths are blocked so that the only color you see is green. This is why colors seem to "change" when we view them in different light, if you are viewing the flyer under light other than white you may get a flawed impression of what the "true" color is.

So if our monitors display in RGB and we're designing for print *how do we really know if our colors will come out as expected?* There are ways to calibrate your monitor to better represent how colors will look on paper but if you always use CMYK mode in your design programs you'll get a good idea of how colors will show up on paper.

Pantone colors (PMS colors) are specific spot ink colors. When we print with Pantone colors we physically put that color ink into the press, instead of blending Cyan, Magenta, Yellow, and Black ink. It's kind of like going to the paint shop and picking "Fenway Park Green" paint. The system exists so a printer in Los Angeles and a printer in Boston can be given the same PMS color code for their printing and it will come out the same.

The Pantone company produces several tools which make it easy to match those colors when you are using Corel Draw or Illustrator to design on your computer. But I warn you not to rely on your program's conversion for an exact match. The same goes for your monitor. Only your local printer can get you the exact matches.

I know the numbers of my logo colors.
◯ YES   ◯ NO

"There are only three colors, ten digits, and seven notes;
it's what we do with them that's important."
Jim Rohn

"Pink isn't just a color, it's an attitude!"
Miley Cyrus

50

Your Employees Are a Different Brand of Customer

There is an old song by Simon and Garfunkle called "Keep the Customer Satisfied." For this tip, we want to consider your employees as customers. Employees are your first line of defense when it comes to protecting your sales numbers. It is important that you understand what really matters to them

Make sure those little feel-good perks actually hit home. Use surveys, focus groups, and interviews to get information about the rewards that matter. For some employees, it's about money. Others are delighted by an evening out on the boss's dime, or when they're treated to lunch. Earning a half-day off or the ability to have some flexibility in work time, when possible, can also be powerful ways to keep employees motivated to perform.

No work environment is perfect, but being happy at work isn't so hard. It just takes some mental fine-tuning.

I treat my clients like family and my employees like clients.
◯ YES   ◯ NO

"It's the same old story
Everywhere I go, I get slandered, libeled
I hear words I never heard in the Bible
And I'm one step ahead of the shoe shine
Two steps away from the county line
Just trying to keep my customers satisfied, satisfied."
Simon and Garfunkle

51

Fill in the _____.

Your goal is to engage your audience. On social media it is done with photos and by asking questions. One of the best tactics is to ask your audience to fill in the blanks. Let's try it here:

My work life summed up in a hashtag is # _____.

My favorite holiday is _____.

The one word that best describes my job is _____.

I should have _____ yesterday.

Everyone should take time to _____ at least once.

Along these lines, I have found that if I leave blanks on the page of my handout people pay closer attention, for example:

- What are the most _____ products I sell?
- In the past twelve months, my bread and butter consumers could be _____ by target market as_____?
- I need to work on enhancing, concentrating or _____ my marketing message by_____.

(*By the way, the fill ins are: profitable, defined, and revising.*)

As I read this book I see I need help with:

_____

_____

_____

_____

"Whenever you find yourself on the side of the majority,
it is time to pause and reflect."
Mark Twain

"Nature abhors a vacuum
but why do most people hasten to fill in the blanks with garbage?"
Vanna Bonta

52

Is Anybody and Everybody on The Phone?
a Demographic Marketing Exercise

Anybody and everybody are not calling you. Your customer is. And identifying the correct demographics of your customers will go a long way towards insuring your success.

Some demographics are obvious; take location. 80% of the business a dry cleaner gets is from a circle three miles in diameter. For a local restaurant it is five to ten miles. The Los Angeles Dodgers and California-Anaheim-Los Angeles Angels of Disneyland both claim all of Southern California. Though truth be told, the line is somewhere between them in Northern Orange County, and the San Diego Padres want part of the state, too.

Some demographics are not so obvious. Sex of the user can be obvious or difficult to determine. Who uses the most makeup products? Who uses bankruptcy attorneys the most? (I'll give ya that one; female professionals a few years out of college who don't use their credit cards very well, and men in their fifties who have lost a job). Can you guess who buys more ties? I'll give you a hint; it's not the people who wear most of them.

There are several other demographics which should be considered when preparing your targeted messages: income, occupation, and how often they need to use your product are all important. In ethnically diverse areas like large cities, race/ethnicity can be important, especially when a city (like Los Angeles) can be seen as a combination of many small communities brought together by freeways and major thoroughfares. Also to be considered is how easy is it to refer to you, and for that surveys written in a certain way can be used as a marketing tool (with apologies to all my public relations courses, surveys can be used in more ways than to gather information).

This is a story about four people: Everybody, Somebody, Anybody, and Nobody.

There was an important job to be done and Everybody was asked to do it.

Everybody was sure Somebody would do it.

Anybody could have done it, but Nobody did it.

Somebody got angry about that because it was Everybody's job.

Everybody thought Anybody could do it, but Nobody realized that Everybody wouldn't do it.

It ended up that Everybody blamed Somebody when actually Nobody asked Anybody.

I realize that everybody is not my client.
○ YES   ○ NO

"You must take personal responsibility.
You cannot change the circumstances, the seasons, or the wind,
but you can change yourself. That is something you have charge of."
Jim Rohn

53

Is E-mail Still an Effective Marketing Tool?

When putting together a marketing plan for a client, a very important question in the two-hour intake interview is "Tell me all the ways in which you market."

Quite often, one of the first answers I get is that the client does mass e-mailings to clients. The answer to the follow up question "How often" can vary greatly from once a day to once a quarter. The next question is the killer and usually begins a discussion: "How effective is it?"

The answer, of course, is almost always that "it depends on the offer," or "we don't know" but what I have noticed and what triggered this tip was an article I once read in the *Boston Globe* by Michael Farrell (March 29, 2013) that e-mail marketing has lost a lot of its effectiveness.

I do not know about you, but I receive upwards of 250–400 e-mails a day. The bulk of them are flat out spam or offers from my promotional product factories with offers that are not all that special. And that is one of the key points I want to stress here.

There are tons of services that have sold us on the idea that e-mail marketing is the best, most effective marketing tool in the world . . . still. It's not that it is ineffective—it is, but for years now, it's been overused. Whether it is a traditional copy-only, e-mail or video filled or packed with hundreds of hyperlinks ready to absorb your prospect's credit card numbers, you have to realize that you are competing with hundreds of thousands of other companies for attention. And even more importantly, you are competing with yourself.

For your e-mail marketing to be effective, you are going to have to use the same rules as direct-mail advertising! When we "drip market" on prospects, we want the offer to make them pause and take notice or we will lose them quickly. Let's use restaurants as an example. If you have a favorite Chinese restaurant, one that gives you consistently good food and service, how much of a special would a competitor have to offer you to get you to try their establishment? 5%? 10% or 25%? Something free? They are asking you to change a habit and that is a difficult thing to do with a prospect.

Similarly, if it is our warm market, how often are we going to walk that tight rope between informing, and flat out selling to current clients? I don't want to be considered a pest. I want people see my Promotionally Minded e-mail and put it on the "gotta open" list.

Let's put ourselves on the receiving side of that equation and decide. One problem with developing an effective e-mail marketing plan is that most of the salespeople selling the systems are just trying to make a dollar and masquerade as "Internet marketing experts." They show you how to use their system, but their messages are muddled. The term "targeted market" means nothing to them because it is all about trying to get the law of large numbers working for you. This is the reason I am not a huge user of mass e-mails. I would rather send the occasional e-mail to a client with a targeted special that makes them take notice.

What kind of offer can you make with your e-mail that will make your prospect think it is so special that the effectiveness speaks for itself? There is a balance you must strike combining the offer, the time frame between mailings, and the markets you are targeting. And I would suggest you narrow your list to those who really fit the target. Even then, you should test several messages by sending a "pre-mail" to a limited number of prospects.

Our e-mail marketing is generating new business.
○ YES   ○ NO

"I don't tweet, Twitter, e-mail, Facebook, look book, no kind of book. I have a land line phone at my home—that's the only phone I have. If my phone rang every day like everyone else around me, I would lose my mind."
Patti LaBelle

54

Discounting

People have the belief that if you put something on sale it will always be on sale. It makes it difficult to take the products off sale.

When I was working for a direct-mail company, I had a client that sold waterbeds. We would rotate the same eight or so bed styles every week, but change the type of sale. Whichever holiday was close (Pre-Labor Day, Labor Day, Labor Day extended) was the headline. Then there were clearances. Or the "Free with Every Purchase" package. But the prices barely changed in four years. The idea of the ads was to get them into the store where the sales team would be happy to give them the advertised bed and mattress at the sale price, but for a few dollars more they would get a much *better* mattress. And for a bit more, they could get a light kit to go with the headboard. And for just a little bit *more*, they could have a six-drawer dresser under the bed instead of the regular base.

In the promotional-products industry there are certain products for which we are never able to get a decent margin. The basic 11 oz. white coffee mug, business card magnets, and simple stick pens are all at the commodity level. It is difficult to add value. What products or services of yours are not as profitable as they could be? Do you want to keep offering them?

It is ok to run specials. I do it all the time on Facebook to attract attention but I change it up. Another concept is to give an unexpected free thing (*term for the unexpected*) which will make a happy customer feel you went above and beyond.

You can even add a special offer inside your invoices. "Here is a special offer only reserved for our best clients."

**I realize the exceptional value I bring to my clients
and can easily express it.**
◯ YES   ◯ NO

"Sometimes I lie awake at night and ask 'Why me?'
Then a voice answers 'Nothing personal,
your name just happened to come up.'"
Charlie Brown, in Charles M. Schulz cartoon Peanuts

55

Testimonials Are Good

When you do a good job, exceed expectations, people are going to tell you they are happy. Having these positive feelings recorded is very important. It is called Social Proof and you can never have enough of it. *Important*: Note that I said *recorded*; not in print.

A short while ago, I put together a marketing plan for a mortgage company. The owner was very happy and *ebulliently* told me so.

My answer to him and everyone else who gives me a complement is to say "That was very kind of you. Is there any way I can have you say that on a short video so I may help other people?" After they do the video, I ask them very nicely to do it one more time. I was taught, and found it to be true, that the second take is almost always better.

So why video instead of a written version? Let me answer that question with a question for you. Have you ever read a testimonial on a website or a pamphlet that said something like "It was the best ever.— Janice H." It is kind of difficult to picture that person or believe it.

A picture says a thousand words but video paints a Technicolor picture of truth. So what do you ask them to say? Here is one formula. It is called the *Before-Now formula*. This script shows a cause and effect relationship where you are the problem solver.

"I am so excited to be a client of Our Marketing Guy. *Before* we began working with that company our marketing was tangential, moving from one project to another without cohesiveness. *Now*, we have a plan that sends all of our efforts in the same direction. My name is Susy Smith from Acme Industry Supply."

Here is one more tip. When shooting the video, you should have a Cheat Card to hold up next to the camera, so your client can easily read it. The card will have this information on it:

"Hello, My Name Is _____

I work / own _____

I want to tell you about Hank Yuloff of OurMarketingGuy.com

I just attended the Our Marketing Guy Boot Camp and it was

_____ .

I just worked with Our Marketing Guy on a marketing plan and it is _____ .
Hard working.
Insightful.
Really knows marketing.
You should work with him to if you want _____."

Have one for different events that you go to. It will help take the nervousness out of your clients.

So, go shoot video. More is better and upload it to your YouTube channel.

I actively pursue video testimonials from clients who mention we have done good work for them.
◯ YES   ◯ NO

"It is amazing how much you can accomplish when it doesn't matter who gets the credit."
Anonymous

56

Be Someone with Whom People Want to Connect

All things being equal, people want to do business with friends. All things *not* being equal, people *still* want to do business with friends. In a networking situation, you don't want to be the person in the room that makes everyone roll their eyes and go out of their way to avoid. At a backyard BBQ, would you give your card to everyone and make sure that they know what you do? Of course not. Or you better not be doing that. Be the talent scout in the room. Look for people who should be connected with others, and bring them together.

I have a friend who says to look for "the Yappers." These are the people who know everyone and who people naturally navigate towards. You should also make sure that the organizer of the event knows you are there, because you want to ask them if there is anything you can do to help make the event more successful.

Here are several ways to build that connectivity:

1. Show up prepared and be ready 100% of the time.

2. Be friendly. Smile. Be open to people coming up to you.

3. Be confident and present. Always look people in the eye.

4. Show interest in them; don't focus on your motives.

5. Find commonality as soon as possible. There is a pneumonic device called F.O.R.M. It stands for Family, Occupation, Recreation, Message. If you are the type who does not know how to make small talk, just keep asking questions that have to do with the first three letters. The Message part is what you leave them with: "hey, we should connect up later. Let's exchange cards." At no time during this conversation, have you forgotten #4 on this list.

6. Give more value than people expect to receive. When people ask me marketing questions, I always answer them.

7. Communicate with excellence

8. Be authentic and be yourself.

9. Avoid alcohol in a business setting. *Everyone* remembers the person who got drunk at that event. It will never reflect well and the story will live forever.

10. The more powerful the connection, the slower the process can be; and that is good.

I look for ways to connect people.
◯ YES ◯ NO

"Truly great friends are hard to find, difficult to leave, and impossible to forget."
Some meme I saw on the Internet.

57

Tradeshow 101: Deciding If You Want to Exhibit

Trade show. Mental images of huge buildings filled with an entire industry worth of *stuff*. The movies have them filled with bikini-clad women luring hangover-nursing businessmen into signing large purchase orders.

The reality of a trade show is generally quite different. For the exhibitors who work the show, it means arriving a day early to set up, long hours standing in a booth, feet that hurt, and trying to differentiate good potential leads from the lookie-loos, and to find great leads among the interested.

For the people who walk the show, it is figuring out how to spend your time wisely, setting goals, and meeting them.

I love trade shows. I love working them. I love walking them.

To me, it is a great way of sharpening my sales abilities and honing the message. It is a great way to make hundreds of cold calls in a single day.

I believe there are good shows for almost every business. Some are local day-long table tops (you get a six- to eight-foot table to display what you do), and some are several-day long-booth shows (you are on a 10' x 10' stage to present your wares).

The key is to pick the correct show to attend. Ask the promoters, "Who will be walking past my booth?"

Like any marketing project, your trade show exhibit will have to be targeted. Who is attending? Are they in your demographic group? Or are *enough* of them going to be in your target demographic to make it worth it? Here is an example: As a marketing company creating incredible marketing plans to develop more business for my clients, I would not exhibit at a Brides to Be show, because "soon-to-be-married couples" are not my target. If I wanted to specialize in gifts that couples gave out at their wedding, I would take my promotional products company, Promotionally Minded, out for a spin and set up my booth with lots of gifts that couples have given out (photo mugs, playing cards, engraved personalized pens) to the people who made their weddings possible. But the question is, how large a bang for my buck will I get for that?

And here is another tip: Some companies have what may be termed as an *open house* for their clients. If you change your mindset and think of it as a *personal trade show*, you may have just created an event that sells. Promotionally Minded does one of these every year and though it is *a lot* of work, it is very worth it.

Deciding on exhibiting at a show is usually a pretty easy decision, but I am going to try and make it easier for you. The next three chapters are going to take you through Trade Show 102, 103, and 104: What to do *before, during,* and very importantly, *after* the trade show to get the most out of them.

I will find local tradeshows which will work for our company.
○ YES   ○ NO

"There's no business like (trade) show business!"
Hank Yuloff

58

Tradeshow 102: Getting Ready for Your Tradeshow

In Tradeshow 101 we discussed the rationale to exhibit at trade shows of various kinds, whether they are full-booth shows or simple table tops where you get a six- or eight-foot table with a tablecloth and a couple of chairs. So let's say we have made the decision to spend the money and go gather some new customers.

Now what?

There are three steps: Get people to your booth, plan who is going to work the show, plan the setup of the booth. We are going to go over some basics for each.

Get people there: It is always fun to see a familiar face when you are working a show. So call your clients, and your prospects. Offer an incredible special if they show up. Because I own a promotional product company, I lean heavily toward making that special a useful and needed gift that carries my logo, but there are lots of ways one can go with this. Use your phone, e-mails, Facebook, and bill stuffers. Start as early as you can and get them there. It is a great way to develop a stronger relationship with clients while showing them new ideas that will help them. You may even consider a contest to get people to show up.

Who is going to work the show: One person rarely gets the job done. At most shows there is too much traffic for one person to handle. You do not want to lose business because you were deeply involved with one prospect when another one comes along. For a table top, two is usually okay. For a 10' x 10' booth, you are better off with at least three. Depending on the number of people expected, and the size of your company, it is good to have someone from different departments to answer possible questions. And depending on where the show is, some shows may seem like a reward.

Ready for the most important note? If you have a table top with two chairs set up behind the table, do *not* let me catch you sitting behind that table, looking up at all the people walking by your table on the way to other tables where there are people standing up and paying attention to the prospects walking by.

Plan the setup of the booth: You just paid for one hundred square feet—use them. Many people think they have to invest thousands of dollars in a trade show booth. Though I sell those, I do not necessarily recommend them. There is a less expensive way. If you sell products, get large photos of your product or photos that demonstrate your service that can be hung on the walls. This allows you to be more flexible in the design, depending upon the show. Remember to make your logo and website prominent. I would suggest you use a table cloth and stand up banners. They are economical and easy to transport. When I train business owners to exhibit at shows, I include a few photos of booths as examples in their training package. If you head to the Our Marketing Guy blog you can find some examples. You will need a strong call to action to get people into your booth. As I mentioned, specials or contests are great. And do not forget a flyer and *plenty* of promotional products that tie into your message. There are tons of ideas, and if you want some, contact me and we can talk about them. Use the super-secret e-mail address we have included at the end of the book

I have a great idea for how to make our tradeshow booth more exciting.
◯ YES ◯ NO

"Hey, don't forget to pack comfortable shoes."
Hank Yuloff

59

Tradeshow 103: During the Show, It Is Game Time, Everybody!

So, you have decided it is a good idea to exhibit at a trade show. Then you found one where the people coming by your booth matches your target demographics. You have ordered promotional products (from Promotionally Minded, of course), brochures and signage (again, from Promotionally Minded) with plenty of time to spare. You know who is going to work the event and what they are going to wear (clothing with your logo on it that matches the banners and give-aways from Promotionally Minded).

Now, it's the day of the show . . . *game time.*

You are about to make several hundred cold calls. Show up early. We recently worked a show and fifteen minutes before "kick off" a bunch of exhibitors were not there yet. They became "Five-Minute Wanders" because they ambled in as the show was opening. They lost the time to settle into their environment and feel comfortable. More importantly, they lost the opportunity to network with their fellow vendors. Vendors who could send them business. (I was able to send three leads to a banker friend who I spoke with prior to the event. I asked him what he was looking for and when I recognized *his* target, I passed off the lead. Why? Not just from the goodness of my heart, but it made me look better to the brand new clients I *was* meeting.)

I probably should not have to say this, but be happy to be there. Smile. Turn off your phone during the show. This is not the time to be checking e-mails. Stand in front of your table, do not hide behind it. There is a psychological disadvantage to be sitting below the people who are checking you out. Your entire job is to get those people to step over the invisible line that runs down the aisle and into your booth or to spend time at your table. If you are out front, you have a much higher chance of making that happen.

If you use signage, be sure that it is readable, especially from a distance. Also, think about people approaching from different directions. Make sure you don't take shortcuts.

At many shows, you may see current clients. During the trade show is a great time to collect video testimonials. Stand your client up against your banner and shoot! It doesn't need to be long. It just needs to be sincere.

Your job during the show is to collect leads. Gather information. Set appointments. Selling is great, but unless you have plenty of staff, you don't want to scare off the prospect. Besides, in the time it takes to fill out that long information form, you could have spoken to a dozen more prospects.

Another important point: Just like a basketball game is forty-eight minutes long and a football game is sixty, you do not want to leave the game with time on the clock. Many sales and connections are made in those last few minutes. You paid for them; get the most out of them. I know your feet hurt and it has been a long day, but tough it out and go for it. Have a contest to see who can get the most leads—and the last lead!

My team is fully trained in how to work a trade show.
◯ YES ◯ NO

"Hi, how are you? My name is Hank. . . .
Hi, how are you,? My name is Hank. . . .
Hi, how are you? My name is Hank. . . . Hi . . ."
Hank Yuloff

60

Tradeshow 104: What Do We Do after the Tradeshow?

Your feet hurt, your back is sore, and you have just spent the day shaking hands with dozens upon dozens of prospects at your trade show booth. So now what? What do you do after the trade show?

This stack of business cards, lead forms, and projects to follow up on was the whole point of the show so you need to get to work.

The first step is to enter all the leads into the Customer Relationship Management System. I prefer Mothernode; it offers many easy-to-use features that other CRM systems do not. My favorite feature is that you can add a web form to everything I put on the Internet. But there are dozens of CRMs.

The purpose of a CRM is to track your leads from the trade show and for every sales situation in which you find yourself. I have gone from follow up by rubber-banded cards to electronically learning and tracking where my business comes from. It will eventually help me track which of my business activities work the best, and which events like a trade show we have been will bring about the most profit to my bottom line. You can try out the CRM system at www.EasyFollowUpTool.com.

Once you have put your trade show leads into the CRM, you need to take a good look at them.

Take care of the 911 leads first. These are the ones who said "Wow, I need you now," or, "Call me tomorrow." It sounds obvious, but there is a huge percentage of trade show leads that go uncalled on, not followed up for many reasons including life getting in the way. Studies show that many leads do not get followed up on because not enough information is captured or the people they give the leads to simply do not consider them important. *They are*; so first things first.

You should take care of the hottest leads first because lots of the other trade show leads will not be as "warm" as you thought. Some people may say one thing when they walk by your trade show booth, but their mind changes quickly after you are out of sight.

I would suggest that if you are a direct-mail-using business, you have your letters ready to go so that all you have to do is add the name and stamp. My company sends out a real greeting card to each person who gives us an address. For about $1.10 (including postage) I get my message over my actual signature into the hands of the trade show attendees, inviting them to do business with my company. Remember, it takes upwards of seven contacts to acquire a new customer so let your thank-you card be one of them.

The ideal time period to get in touch with your leads is within two business days so in advance of your show mark your calendar to keep your schedule open.

For all the leads, it is time to get on the phone and make some calls! Give them an offer they cannot refuse! Get that new business!

We are using tradeshows to our benefit.

◯ YES ◯ NO

"Willingness to change is a strength, even if it means plunging part of the company into total confusion for a while."
Jack Welch

61

A Trick to Generating Leads
with Social Media

If a neighbor came over for five days straight and brought a pie, wouldn't you start to feel you owed them something?

Promoting others on Facebook brings a huge reciprocity. The positive attitude you show by telling a good story about some work that has been done for you or your company reflects back on you.

When you make a new connection on social media one of the best questions you can ask them is to tell you more about themselves. Ask what they do for fun. After one or two exchanges, say, "I'm a bad typist; can we just jump on the phone?" The goal is to move a connection from being virtual online to real offline.

**Before I read the next chapter,
I am going to go promote someone on social media.**
◯ YES   ◯ NO

———————————————

"In times of rapid change, experience could be your worst enemy."
J. Paul Getty

"Don't be afraid to change the model."
Reed Hastings

62

Hi, My Name Is Hank Yuloff and I Am a Technophobe

It's not because I hate technology; it's great. But the human mind, okay *my* human mind, gets comfortable with a certain level of what these computer thingys can do, and the kind of websites and web tools that are available when all of a sudden . . . *wham* we have a whole new bunch of new toys.

In the past, I was very slow to use them (can't tell you how many people have heard my "e-mail is never going to be important" speech), but lately I have been getting better and in a couple of ways, my company has gotten ahead of the curve. It has allowed us to leverage our time—make better use of that time—by using technology to "bend time" and get more done.

So let's talk about one tool that is pretty ubiquitous and incredibly useful but technophobes like me, who are not trying to reform, avoid it like a plague of technological locusts.

It's Facebook and all the other social media sites.

If you are on that site and are using it to generate a bit of business, this post is not for you. Or, if you are on Facebook but think it is just for posting cute photos of your dog, maybe this post *is* for you.

If business is about making connections, then Facebook is *all* about business. And it is an incredible tool for it.

One day, I saw a friend ask for connections to buy a new SUV. I was not able to *easily* connect her to someone in one of my networking groups, because she is not in my area. I *did* connect her through e-mail to an acquaintance, but the extra promotion that she would have gotten if I could have highlighted her link on Facebook would have been a very *good thing*. And in the time it took me to make my connection, two people were able to make that very public connection ahead of me.

A couple of mornings later, I had breakfast with an incredible connector. His primary business is life insurance, but his main marketing strategy is to connect two people every day before lunch. I would highlight him but he is not on Facebook. He told me he got angry that someone else put him on LinkedIn and he is very happy to be in just one networking group that frowns on direct solicitation of people in your group (referring members meet in groups of two or three to get to know each other better and develop personal relationships). That is effective. And at two to three people at a time . . . *slow*. Glacially slow.

Here is my alternative. If I was able to stand up in front of a chamber of commerce breakfast networking meeting and say, "Hey, everyone, this insurance guy is an incredibly caring life-insurance salesperson. You should call him and get to know him better. Let me give you his number," that could be pretty effective. And a bit faster than his way; just for that one mention . . . where half of my audience may or may not be listening to me.

Is that as effective as me putting it in my blog, which is also going to be on the OurMarketingGuy.com blog and pushed out to a couple of dozen other places and then shared onto my Facebook pages several times?

I hope I am preaching to a choir here, but perhaps you can point this chapter out to one of your, "I don't have time for Facebook" friends. And while you are at it, please let them know how incredible the rest of this book is.

I am comfortable with technology or know someone who can assist me.
◯ YES   ◯ NO

"The people who resist change will be confronted by the growing number of people who see that better ways are available; thanks to technology."
Bill Gates

63

Why Do I Blog?

Let's discuss the *why* first. It used to be that when someone referred you to a friend, the only way to check you out was for them to check out your brochure that they had been handed and then to meet with you in person and check out the "cut of your jib." Now, they can go online and get to know you before they even call.

Social media and your website are how people pre-sell themselves on you. Your website is a lot more than a brochure; it is a complete press kit. So if your website is not as good as your competitors, it counts against you. Your blog is a big part of that. By having a blog that is constantly being updated, you are able to let that prospect get to know you before you are in the same room.

The other two reasons to blog are to create organic search engine optimization. This is accomplished in two ways. The first is your way of showing the major search engines that because your website is constantly changing you are invested in the Internet and you believe that the Internet is a great way to do business. When someone types key words that match what you do, a search engine has mere moments to decide whether to put your website on the top or a competitor. If your website changes twice a week, and your competitor blogs once a quarter, guess which website will show up first?

When we write blogs for our clients, we naturally use terms associated with their industry. And when I write blogs for OurMarketingGuy.com, I use terms like marketing plans, promotional products, logo development, and digital assets all the time. So when someone types those words into the search window, the search engine sees that I am very invested in the Internet and I am talking about what my new potential client is looking for so they have a better chance of matching us up.

Key point: I strongly suggest that you shoot videos to accompany as many of your blogs as possible. When we do a marketing plan for a client, we set up their YouTube channel as a place for their videos to live. At the writing of this book, YouTube channels are free so there is zero reason not to create one. Search engines love video and reward it because posting videos along with your blog is harder than just writing the blog.

To review: Blogging is worth the hour of your time it may take because it is an inexpensive way improve your search engine optimization.

I am a blogging machine!
◯ YES   ◯ NO

"The speed of the leader determines the speed of the pack."
Wayne Lukas

*"Sometimes, I think my most important job as a CEO is to listen for bad news.
If you don't act on it, your people will eventually stop bringing bad news
to your attention and that is the beginning of the end."*
Bill Gates

64

How Do I Blog?

The first step is to pick a topic. You might want to make a list of several because the more you have on your list, the more eager you are to get them written. I like to write them in bunches.

The second step is to make a few notes about what you want to include in the blog. If you are not used to writing, or have not written in a long while, here is a simple formula.

Your first paragraph is your statement of truth. The next two to three paragraphs have two or three sentences each and are the supporting statements for your statement of truth, with one fact per paragraph. Then the last paragraph reviews what you just wrote about.

Does this sound like your high school English teacher? It should, because that is what they were teaching you in school, to blog. But they thought they were teaching you to write book reports and current events in a short, concise manner. They were also quick to read and grade, but that is just another point.

Some people like to write their blogs by shooting it as a two minute video first and then transcribing it. I'm one of those people and highly suggest using this method. In fact, when we go on vacation, I take my lists of blogs to be written and shoot them as videos in unusual places—places where the regular watchers and readers of my blog do not normally see me. I want my clients to know that I may be going to Hawaii or Sedona or on a cruise ship, but their business success is never far from my mind. You should place this video at the top of your blog right under the headline.

Your headline should be key-word friendly and describe what is in the blog. I try and make them fun.

Then place your written blog right under the video.

If you do not use a video, then I suggest you use a photo that ties in with it. People like pictures.

At the bottom of my blogs, I always include a webform so that when people want more information on the subject, they know how to instantly get in touch with me.

Key point: If you are in the process of developing your website, I suggest you use a Word Press theme to put it together. The blog pages are almost identical to a Word document, and it makes it very easy to insert YouTube video embed codes, links to websites, and photographs.

Because I got As and Bs in English classes, I am awesome at blogging.
◯ YES ◯ NO

"Don't focus on having a great blog.
Focus on producing a blog that's great for your readers."
Brian Clark

"I think the pleasure of completed work is what makes blogging so popular.
You have to believe most bloggers have few if any actual readers.
The writers are in it for other reasons.
Blogging is like work, but without coworkers thwarting you at every turn.
All you get is the pleasure of a completed task."
Scott Adams

65

What Do I Write about in My Blog?

First of all, when I tell you to blog, I am not looking for you to write a book. You are reading a book right now. It may not be *War and Peace*, but it is a book. A blog is more like writing in your diary. Put one hundred diary entries together and you *have* a book, but let's start small.

Your blog is going to be between three hundred and six hundred words. If you want an example of 445 words, look at this chapter.

Here are things that make your blog useful to both you and your clients...

1. There are a lot of questions clients always ask you. These are your first ten blog posts. Here are a couple of examples. When I put together a marketing plan for a business, they always ask me how they should be prepared for our meetings. That's a blog post. They also ask me how to get ready to exhibit at trade shows. That is four more blog posts, which are included in this book.

2. There are a lot of questions you *want* clients to ask you. Those are the next ten blog posts.

3. You can interview people relevant to your industry and turn it in to a blog. Ask three or four questions, then add a paragraph at the beginning on why you interviewed them and another one at the end that wraps up what was said. The easiest way to do this is as a Google Hangout. After you finish, you can just quickly transcribe what was said and your blog will have both a video and written version. That is *gold*!

4. Find two or three related quotes on a subject and share your feelings about them.

5. Swap blog space with friends—they guest blog in your blog space, and you on theirs. It allows you to repurpose (get extra use from) a blog post that you have already posted on your own website.

6. Review someone's book. Hey, here's an idea—review *this* book in your blog. Then send an e-mail to WeLove@OurMarketingGuy.

com. If you do, I may interview you for my blog, which will create more back links to your website which is good.

7. Review someone's blog posts or videos. I would suggest you do 95% positive reviews while feeling free to add your opinions on what was said in their blog. *Always* use a link back to their blog.

8. On my OurMarketingGuy.com blog, I *love* taking items that I find in the news and do some current-events marketing where I discuss the event and how it affects my industry, my clients' businesses, or how people can take the same news event to market themselves.

9. *Very important note*: As I was writing this book, a change was taking place in the world of search engines. Every few times you blog, you should produce a blog that is over a thousand words long. It will be considered to have more depth.

I have created a list of blog topics and am continually adding to it.
◯ YES   ◯ NO

"There are no working hours for leaders."
James Cardinal Gibbons

"The ability to deal with people is as purchasable as a commodity as sugar or coffee and I will pay more for that ability than for any other thing under the sun."
John D. Rockefeller

66

Sales Opportunities: a Ten-Things-to-Remember List

People will switch when the pain of changing is less than the pain of staying. You job is to tell them what their pain is and how to solve the problem. You have to know about your clients. You have to know why they have bought through someone else.

10. Know who you are. Don't try to be something you're not. If you're not going to win; don't spend the time.

9. Be really good at something. Make *sure* they know who you are and what you're good at.

8. It is your goal to be different than your competition.

7. Create a realistic *target list* and update it constantly.

6. Be prepared and always continue to learn.

5. Continuing research is your key to success. Searching for that key that will help you win. It is okay to fight "dirty" by knowing more.

4. Get creative in your continuous contact with clients and prospects.

3. Pursue methods and skills that your competition is lacking.

2. You will have to take clients away from someone else. Prepare—prepare—prepare.

1. Make the plan; and work it. You do not have to fail because the state of the economy is good or bad. You have to do a better job of preparing.

I go into every sales opportunity fully prepared.
◯ YES   ◯ NO

"Appreciation will win out over self-promotion every time."
Kody Bateman

"Create your own Stimulus Program."
Hank Yuloff

"The process of closing a sale doesn't start after you complete your presentation, it begins when you walk into the door, when you shake your prospect's hand."
Joe Buzzello

67

Ten plus One Ways to Use Promotional Products

The worst thing that could happen to these marketing tools is the *best* thing that could happen to other advertising . . . that's if you were to read it and then throw it away. But if you don't just read it and throw it away, you will have an enjoyable and useful tool to lighten and brighten your home or office. When promotional products are used properly, they are a useful and needed tool which will garner appreciation from the giver.

Here are ten plus one reasons to use promotional products:

1. One of the most common questions we ask each other is ,"What's new?" So when you have something new happening in your business, promote it! A new office, location or store. A new phone number or area code change. If you have a new or updated website along with a change in your e-mail address. Putting this information on a useful promotional product will keep this information at your client fingertips.

2. Use them to introduce a new product or a new service. These introductions and beginnings are very important to your company. Maybe it involves a name change, a new addition, new people promoted to handle this new offering. Whatever it is, those who are buying what you sell need to know about it, and remember it. You can also use promos to introduce new people in your organization to your clients. The people who connect with your customers the most need to be recognized for their good work and recognized when your clients call.

3. Having a motivated and inspired team is important to your sales efforts. It can be anyone on the team: Sales, shipping, office, production, customer service, or even independent reps. People respond to appreciation and outreach so whether it is a sales meeting, product launch or to announce a safety program, using a promotional product to keep these programs in mind will help you.

4. Use them to motivate and reward your clients and prospects. Promotional products encourage them to take the actions you want them to take. We want to reward the positive and build goodwill. Everyone likes to receive a gift; you'll benefit when you give one to your customers. This also covers those free-gift-with-purchase situations.

5. You can use promotional products as an incentive for people to take an action or talk to you. I entered 5k runs and gave blood because they were giving away a t-shirt. Sending the promotional product in a box or mailing tube will attract attention and gain you enough face time with the prospect to generate *real* face to face time. I recently had a florist client who gave imprinted pens to one of their wholesalers (with the wholesaler's name on it) as a thank you for their good service and to generate good will. The recipient was overjoyed and my client has received far more value than what they paid for the pens.

6. Your marketing goal is to create an image, build awareness, and demonstrate your abilities while positioning your company as "top of mind" so when your service is needed, you are literally within an arm's length.

7. Traffic. In your retail store, at an open house, passing your trade show booth, you want people to beat a path to your door. The promo can be mailed in advance, hand delivered, or offered on location when they show up. I have had clients mail a single playing card to prospects saying to bring it to their trade show booth for the complete deck.

8. Customers sometimes drift away. Let's remind them that you exist and reactivate their accounts. I have had clients who offered company jackets, travel first-aid kits, even Android tablets to customers who increased their spending with them quarter to quarter or annually. Offer something extra and many will respond positively.

9. In addition to past clients, we want to open new doors and accounts. There are markets you may not have opened using conventional sales techniques, so reach out with a unique and unusual approach.

10. It could be in response to what a competitor is doing, to sell the rest of a closeout item, to offer a premium for your factory

representatives and dealers, this is a great extra tool. For example offer a pocket knife or flashlight with each case of your product that a wholesaler distributes.

11. Use them to say "thank-you" to anyone—everyone—for any reason. At any time or in any place. What you offer is a demonstration of your caring and appreciation for a job well done. A goal met. For being a leader—or a follower. For being loyal. For walking the extra mile. Or . . . for just being!

We love having our logo positioned all over our client's offices, home, and car.
◯ YES ◯ NO

"Doing business without advertising is like winking at a girl in the dark, you know what you are doing but nobody else does."
Ed Howe

"Every tomorrow has two handles. You can take hold of the handle of anxiety or the handle of enthusiasm. Upon your choice so will be the day."
Brian Tracy

68

Social Media: Five Rules
for Social Media Posts

Have you ever gotten into a SHOUTING MATCH ONLINE WHERE BOTH OF YOU WERE IN CAP LOCK MODE?

It happens quite often. And it usually ends with one party unfriending or in some other way blocking the other person out of their online, virtual life. There are lots of reasons these arguments happen and most of them boil down to one of five categories which should be avoided: sex, religion, politics, sports and negativity.

Why are we, the enlightened business owners, avoiding these topics? Simple. There are two purposes we are on social media: Staying in contact with friends and family, and to do more business.

On the business side, picture your social media (SM) as one very large funnel. In fact, picture all your networking activities as this funnel. Your job is to get as many people into that funnel as possible to build a relationship. When they are in that funnel, they are meeting you, checking you out and finally deciding if they want to drop down through the bottom hole in that funnel and become your customer. Many people will be looking for reasons to do just the opposite and hop *out* of your funnel. Why give them a reason by posting something they think is stupid on your social media accounts? Here is why we avoid these five catagories:

Sex: No one cares what you are doing in your bedroom. And unless they include lots of photos and video, you probably do not care what other people are doing in their bedroom. Or with whom. Whether you are straight or gay, pushing your sexual preferences is one way to eliminate a potential client.

Religion: I see people post biblical verses and other religious comments all the time. Sometimes I read them. And sometimes I actually like the comment. But 99.999% of the time, these posts seem preachy and 100% of the time posts are not going to convert me or change my religious habits. I have jumped out of lots of funnels because of religious posts.

Politics: Similarly to religion, no matter how logical your argument, you are not going to change the political leanings of anyone. And since the country is split roughly between 50-50% and 40-60% on most issues all you are doing is angering half of your potential audience.

Sports: In Los Angeles two of the major universities do not like each other. For a UCLA Bruin's fan to say that USC sucks is not going to garner them any good will by any Trojan fan who reads it. Same with Ohio State and Michigan. Yankee and Red Sox fans. Dodgers and Giants. Lakers and Celtics. Notre Dame and anyone. Best to avoid this topic.

Negativity: "I am so tired of my neighbor getting up at 8 a.m. in the morning and playing loud music. It wakes me up. Oh, and their pink house makes me think of a Pepto Bismol bottle. And their barking dog wakes up my cat." Ever read posts like this? Makes you want to run screaming, right? This kind of post is why my Facebook page is set up to run four positive posts a day.

Have I broken these rules? Every one of them. But I try to catch myself before I hit *enter*. Here is my favorite post: "All my liberal employees will be required to take a pregnancy test each time they have gay sex prior to a New York Giants game. It will be administered in public by my congregation and we will then pray for their souls."

I am cognizant that the real purpose of social media is to build my business.
○ YES ○ NO

"Everyone has an invisible sign hanging from their neck saying, 'make me feel important.' Never forget this message when working with people."
Mary Kay Ash

69

Social Media: You Need a Business Fan Page

At some point, I have a strong feeling that this section will be completely useless. Social media website services come and go and depending on how effective their ability is to make sales, the longer they will last. That being said, let's talk about social media sites in general and Facebook specifically.

Your personal profile is for your non-commercial use and is your own personal page. Business pages (for companies, organizations and non-breathing entities) look similar to your personal page but offer specific tools to help market those entities. They look similar but where you are "friends" on personal pages, your business page has "fans."

Each person who signs up for Facebook gets one account per name. Each of those accounts can have one personal profile but they can manage many pages.

You can follow profiles to see public updates from people you're interested in but aren't friends with. Pages look similar to personal profiles, but they offer unique tools for businesses, brands, and organizations. Pages are managed by people who have a personal profile. You can like a page to see updates in the news feed.

To summarize: Each person who signs up for Facebook has one account with login information. Each account can have one personal profile and manage multiple pages.

I am talking about this because if you are relying on sites like Facebook to be your company's one or main website or web presence, you need to carefully read the terms of use. Facebook, or other social media sites *own* your pages and if you are using your account for other purposes than to promote yourself or your business, you could lose your access to your personal page. Bottom line is don't do stupid stuff!

The following is from the Facebook terms of use (as of November 2014):

> How are pages different from groups? Which one should I create?

> Pages allow real organizations, businesses, celebrities and brands to communicate broadly with people who like them. Pages may only be created and managed by official representatives.

Groups provide a closed space for small groups of people to communicate about shared interests. Groups can be created by anyone.

Other differences include:

Pages

Privacy: Page information and posts are public and generally available to everyone on Facebook.

Audience: Anyone can like a page to connect with it and get news feed updates. There is no limit to how many people can like a page.

Communication: People who help manage a page can share posts from the page. Page posts can appear in the news feeds of people who like the page. Page owners can also create customized apps for their page and check page insights to track the page's growth and activity.

Groups

Privacy: In addition to a public setting, more privacy settings are available for groups. In secret and closed groups, posts are only visible to group members.

Audience: You can adjust group privacy to require members to be approved or added by administrators. When a group reaches a certain size, some features are limited. The most useful groups tend to be the ones you create with small groups of people you know.

Communication: In groups, members receive notifications by default when any member posts in the group. Group members can participate in chats, upload photos to shared albums, collaborate on group docs, and invite members who are friends to group events.

Our company has an active social media presence.
◯ YES ◯ NO

"How many people are completely successful in every department of life?
Not one. The most successful people are the ones who learn from their mistakes
and turn their failures into opportunities."
Zig Ziglar

70

Using the Internet and Social Media to Track Competitors

Keeping up with what is going on in your industry is always a great idea. There are lots of ways to do that. The most common way is to get involved with organizations that are related to your industry. Show up for their meetings and ask a lot of questions at those meetings.

Slightly less common is to use the Internet to keep an eye on what is going on around you. Let's chat about that just a little bit You should always pay attention to what is going on in your industry and the internet is a great tool.

You need to keep something in mind, here, though. There are times when paying a little bit of attention to your competition is not a bad thing, but you should be far more interested in being so successful that they are trying to see what *you* are doing.

I wanted to give you one more website which will be very useful to you—NameChek.com. It allows you to check the availability of your name on dozens of social media sites.

We are so focused on what we are doing within our business, it makes no difference what our competitors are doing.
◯ YES   ◯ NO

"Don't look back. Something might be gaining on you."
Satchel Paige

71

Vanity Phone Numbers

You see them all the time—vanity license plates on cars and vanity phone numbers in advertisements. Do they work?

I am going to say "yes" but understand that I do not have scientific back up. I've looked for studies on them but found none, so here is my small research study of one: I constantly have clients tell me they have my number memorized and they know all they have to do is remember the first three numbers because *Hank* is who they are calling. Pretty compelling evidence, huh? I have used them for over twenty years. All my numbers end with "-4265" which spells out "-HANK." It began with the 818 version "818-705-4265" and then the fax "(818)789-HANK," then the toll free numbers, and then my cell phone number.

How did I get them? A bit of luck, and lots of patience. I dialed (800)705-4265 every sixty days for years and eventually when it became available I contacted my provider and grabbed it.   You should use numbers that lead into your occupation or your name. For example, if you're a plumber, use "Fast," "Leak," or "Pipe." Keep them to four letters on the right side of the hyphen unless you can get all seven numbers. We've been taught to remember phone numbers in terms of three numbers (area code), then three more numbers (prefix), then four numbers.

The question comes up all the time regarding the value of toll-free numbers. My answer will always be *yes*, you should get one. For a long time, area codes were being split and split again. It makes a lot of sense to let clients know that you are giving them something free from the beginning of your relationship, through the sales presentation, and on to the sale.

The biggest mistake is to use the letter "O" because it is confused with the number zero. The biggest "always" is when you advertise the number always give the actual numbers which are represented by the words—705-HANK is always promoted as 705-HANK (4265). I don't want to anger a customer who doesn't want to look up the number for represented by the letter just for the sake of vanity!

Our phone number is very easy to remember.
○ YES ○ NO

"If it's the Psychic Network, why do they need a phone number?"
Robin Williams

72

Quick Fundraising Ideas for Non-Profits

If you are a non-profit, ask a local business if you can help them increase their Facebook or other social media following. In exchange for bringing more "likes," or more *engagement* to their page, you receive a donation during a specific time period. This makes them look good, too. The business can advertise that they are building their business but doing good in the community at the same time. "Like our page and we will give $1 to an organization that we feel is making our community better. Our goal is to give them $1000 in the next week but we need your help."

Do each of the members of your board of directors have links on their website to the donation page on your website? I spoke in front of a Rotary group and asked this question and it was if I had dropped an OMG Bomb in the room. Not one of them had done this so I am thinking that if a group as dedicated to public service as Rotarians have missed this, I should promote it to all non-profits.

Talk to direct-sales company reps for home parties—you invite friends, they sell products, you get money. Pampered Chef, Scentscy, and Mary Kay reps are all good targets. My fellow SendOutCards reps are taught that showing appreciation is the best thing in the world. Ask them to hold a card party for your group. Tell them I sent ya!

Hugs for Sale! Go to your local mall and give a hug for a donation! If you are fun loving everyone will have a great time for a great cause. For those that are not too keen on a physical hug, give them the option to get a Hershey's candy hug instead. You could even set up a booth like Lucy in *Peanuts* and her charge for her advice for $1 (or more). Any lawyers in your group? This could be a good fundraiser, too.

How do we spell S-U-C-C-E-S-S? Hold a spell-a-thon with each contestant collecting donations for the number of words they spell correctly. The top winners receive donated prizes.

This is a way for a non-profit to share a spotlight with a local school. Members of your board of directors can compete against the students. (I suggest you study hard because they are probably going to beat you.)

The school can sell tickets for admission and keep all the proceeds. Sell drinks and refreshments and split the take. This idea can also be used by one non-profit or chamber of commerce to compete against several schools in one evening.

If you have connections with local restaurants, ask if you can leave a fish-bowl at the front counter. Add a sign that awards a free lunch for the winning cards pulled from the bowl.

For service clubs, invite business owners who drop their cards into the bowl to your weekly meeting. As a tradeoff with the restaurant, your group should pay for the lunch that is won.

I realize that one reason to be in business is to make my community a better place. I can think of three non-profits that I can assist.
◯ YES ◯ NO

"If you can dream it, you can do it."
Walt Disney

"It's never too late to learn."
Malcolm Forbes

"I can accept failure, everyone fails at something.
But I cannot accept not trying."
Michael Jordan

"Be a life-long student, read as many books as possible."
Nelson Mandela

"A real leader faces the music even when he doesn't like the tune."
Arnold H. Glassgow

73

Slogans Wrap You Up in One Short Phrase

Back in my college advertising classes, we were taught to know how to come up with catchy slogans to help promote our clients. The purpose of a slogan is obvious, in a few words to express the benefits of your product or service. You want to immediately put a positive image into your client's mind. Here's an example: "The Happiest Place on Earth." Send me an e-mail if you didn't just have a certain amusement park pop into your head.

Here are ten things to keep in mind when putting your slogan together:

1. Make it memorable. Make it easy to remember, something they want to brand in their memory and possibly even repeat to others. Take for example the following slogans (Make this a game; wherever you are reading this, shout out the advertiser after the slogan. Or if you are on a plane, shout out the slogans and see if people can tell you the company.):

   "Just Do It" Nike (1988)
   "Reach out and touch someone" AT&T
   "Good to the last drop" Maxwell House

2. Your slogan must contain a key benefit of the product or service. It gives people a reason to remember it.

   "Tastes great, less filling" Miller Lite (1975)
   "When it absolutely, positively has to be there overnight."
       Federal Express
   "We Have to Try Harder" Avis (1963)

3. It should be easy to understand when people see it on walking bill-boards (t-shirts or bags).

   "Got Milk?" California Milk Advisory Board (1993)
   "Where's the Beef?" Burger King (1980s)
   "Breakfast of Champions" Wheaties

4. It should differentiate your brand. Does it bring out the character of the product or services that sets it apart from your competitors?

"Diamonds are forever" DeBeers (1938)
"All the News That's Fit to Print" *The New York Times*
"You're in Good Hands with Allstate" Allstate Insurance (1956)

5. It must recall and solidify the brand name no matter who remembers it. The brand can be depicted in the words you use or in the image of your logo. Budweiser uses "The King of Beers" everywhere its logo is used.

"Don't Leave Home without It." American Express (1975)

6. It could be easy to say, like a nursery rhyme. That will help it stick in the memory of everyone who hears it.

"Takes a licking and keeps on ticking." Timex

7. Don't underestimate the warm and fuzzy effect. Does your slogan leave people feeling good all over? Does it bring a smile to their face or perhaps even a little chuckle? A slogan is more likely to stick in the minds of others if it imparts a positive feeling or emotion.

"Melts in Your Mouth, Not in Your Hand" – M&Ms (1954)
"When You Care Enough to Send the Very Best" Hallmark
(but I suggest you go to www.CardsByHank.com
and mail cards for about a dollar including postage.)

8. Keep it Simple. Shorter is usually better.

"Finger lickin' good" KFC
"Drivers Wanted" Volkeswagen
"Intel Inside" Intel

9. Know that sometimes, the slogan will outlive the product!

"Let Your Fingers Do the Walking" Yellow Pages
"Is it live or is it Memorex?" Memorex
"The Fun Develops Instantly" Polaroid

10. Understand that sometimes you will just stumble into it.

I have a unique way of describing my company.
◯ YES ◯ NO

"Our major obligation is not to mistake slogans for solutions."
Edward R. Murrow

"You can't just have slogans, you can't just have catchy phrases. You have to have an agenda."
Colin Powell

74

Fun with Slogans:
Do Not Get Lost in Translation

Just for fun, I am including these Our Marketing Guy advertising issues. They could be urban legends, but when I was putting the book together I found this information (I don't know where it came from but would love to give credit in a subsequent edition) from years ago. It could be a reminder to all of us not to take ourselves so seriously—it's only business! I also thought it might just be an amusing warning that when you are advertising in a language in which you are not fluent, it is probably a good idea . . . a great idea . . . to have two different translation companies take a shot at it for you.

- When Parker Pen marketed a ball-point pen in Mexico, its ads were supposed to have read, "It won't leak in your pocket and embarrass you." The company thought that the word "embarazar" (to impregnate) meant to embarrass, so the ad read: "It won't leak in your pocket and make you pregnant."

- Scandinavian vacuum manufacturer Electrolux used the following in an American campaign: "Nothing sucks like an Electrolux."

- Clairol introduced the Mist Stick, a curling iron, into Germany only to find out that "mist" is slang for manure. Not too many people had use for the "Manure Stick."

- Coors put its slogan, "Turn It Loose," into Spanish, where it was read as "Suffer from Diarrhea."

- Pepsi's "Come Alive with the Pepsi Generation" translated into "Pepsi Brings Your Ancestors Back from the Grave" in Chinese.

- When Gerber started selling baby food in Africa, they used the same packaging as in the US, with the smiling baby on the label. Later they learned that in Africa, companies routinely put pictures of what's inside on the labels, since many people can't read.

- Colgate introduced a toothpaste in France called Cue, the name of a notorious porno magazine.

- Frank Perdue's chicken slogan, "It takes a strong man to make a tender chicken," was translated into Spanish as "It takes an aroused man to make a chicken affectionate."

- When American Airlines wanted to advertise its new leather first-class seats in the Mexican market, it translated its "Fly in Leather" campaign literally, which meant" "Fly Naked" (*vuela en cuero*) in Spanish.

- An American T-shirt maker in Miami printed shirts for the Spanish market promoting the Pope's visit. Instead of "I saw the Pope" (*el Papa*), the shirts read "I saw the potato" *(la papa)*.

- The Dairy Association's huge success with the campaign "Got Milk?" prompted them to expand advertising to Mexico. It was soon brought to their attention the Spanish translation read "Are You Lactating?"

- General Motors had a famous fiasco in trying to market the Nova car in Central and South America. "*No va*" in Spanish means, "It Doesn't Go."

- The Coca-Cola name in China was first rendered phonetically into a word which meant "Bite the Wax Tadpole," or "Female Horse Stuffed with Wax," depending on the dialect. Coke then researched 40,000 characters to find a phonetic equivalent "kekou kele," translating into "Happiness in the Mouth."

**We have a slogan that is part of our marketing efforts.
It's kinda cute, too.**
○ YES ○ NO

---

*"It is better to have read a great work of another culture in translation
than never to have read it at all."*
Henry Gratton Doyle

75

Once You Know Who, You Will Know What

Once you know what, you get to choose how.

Most businesses begin their marketing plans with the *how*. If they start a business in an industry they are familiar with, they do what they did when they worked for someone else. In many client situations I have found that it was the reason the entrepreneur felt comfortable in starting their own company. Then, once they started their business, they were bombarded by dozens of salespeople, each hawking their own product as "the perfect way to get your name out there." Some of them might be, but most of them won't be.

Let's take a nice long walk through over four dozen different ways to market your business and see how they might work for your company.

Very important note here: When choosing different ways to market your business, *always* begin with the end in mind. Why are you using this type of tactic? How is this tactic going to put you in front of your target market. Will this tactic help you with more than one target? Each one of those target markets could have different tactics.

Here are a couple of examples using my own business: I have used my membership in three chambers of commerce to meet business owners in the geographic area closest to our office. Within those chambers, I used different tactics to establish our company as a leader in our industry. I had an opportunity to join a hard-networking group in a different part of Los Angeles, which I took. It opened a new geographic area and seventy new businesses with which I had close to zero contact with previously. When I ran the numbers, cost versus minimum acceptable profits and probable profits, it was worth taking the leap.

In preparing for our Promotionally Minded Marketing Days, we use several methods to target current and potential clients. E-mail, direct mail, personal phone calls, speaking opportunities, and more.

For any one business, there is no silver bullet of perfection. It will take several tactics to successfully market your company. In fact, the more things you do, the more solid your business will become. Imagine a four-foot high director's chair. If you took one of those four legs away, you might be able to balance, but if you took away two, you are going to fall over. If you added more legs, it would make for a much more stable chair.

You have read over a hundred pages and more than seventy chapters to find out who you want to market to, now you get to pick out the tactics that will get you there.

As you go through the list in the next chapter, note which ones you already utilize (and enter them on your personal marketing list which follows on page 160.

If you see ideas which intrigue you, add them on to the list on page 161 and I'll tell you what to do with those, too.

**We know that it makes sense to have at least ten methods
of marketing working for us at all times.**
○ YES   ○ NO

---

*"I am always doing that which I cannot do,
in order that I may learn how to do it."*
Pablo Picasso

76

The List

Use the following list to select the items that you are already doing to market your business. Check off those items that you are not doing, but which interest you and that you might want to try out.

Appreciation. Appreciation wins out over self-promotion every time. Figure out ways to say *thanks* (I always say you can't say *thanks* without *Hank*) to your clients. Gifts, leads, promoting them on social media all are ways that you can stand apart.
◯ I need more of this.

Articles to target clients. When you are reading a magazine or a newspaper or even a news website, you will see articles that make you think of some of your clients. Cut that article out (or print it) and send it to your client with a post it that says, "I read this and thought of you." *Do not* add your brochure or sales sheet. This is just reaching out to a client. I have had lots of clients subscribe to business periodicals or special publications like *The Robb Report* or high-end vehicle magazines for this exact purpose

◯ I need more of this.

Be a connector. Look to add people to your Rolodex and find them business. The more you do this, the more business will come back to you. Someone is always asking for something on social media. Be the one who gets the private message asking you for help. You can even tell people to post their websites on your social media (as long as they click on the link of someone else who has posted).
◯ I need more of this.

Be the bearer of good news. People like to be a part of something big and special. When something awesome happens in your business, let them know. You could be the sponsor of a neighborhood event, speaking at a national conference for your industry. I spoke at the 100th anniversary of my college newspaper event (*TheDailyAztec.com* at San Diego State University) and put it all over my social media. In my company, I have been the Employee of the Month for over two hundred straight months. I create press releases using a famous newspaper header (I say the article *should* appear there) and put it on a greeting card that goes to clients.

○ I need more of this.

Become a celebrity. Part of the benefit of sending regular press releases to local media is that eventually you could be quoted and be on news shows. Create a video that will become part of your website. Celebrity comes in all forms. From one little post that I run every night on a social media site, I have people come up to me constantly.

○ I need more of this.

Become a reporter/local expert. Local and regional publications and broadcast stations are always looking for content. Send examples of your brilliance to these stations. Follow up consistently and maybe you will get a regular gig. But it's usually a free gig.

○ I need more of this.

Birthday program. When I go to chamber meetings I inevitably have someone say, "Hey Hank, thanks for the card." My answer is, "You are welcome; happy birthday!" My SendOutCards system sends real birthday cards to clients. Apart from their family, I am generally the only vendor that remembers their birthday (I ask for them, by the way). For less than a dollar, I stand out.

○ I need more of this.

Celebrity endorsements. Know anyone famous? Get them to say your name on video! Get them to use your product and be seen using it.

○ I need more of this.

Cold calling—walk in. I was chatting recently with a plumber client. He mentioned that he chose a shopping center and just walked in to leave his information along with some cool promotional products. From those twenty or so calls he generated two new clients. Getting out of your office and knocking on doors will always be a great way to get business . . . if you *follow* up.

○ I need more of this.

Cold calling—phone. It's always good to make a few calls. Pick a highly targeted group, so when you are dumped into phone-call voice-mail hell, you have a specific reason for them to call you back. If you are a little hesitant to make calls because of the time it takes, just schedule twenty-two minutes at a time to do it.

○ I need more of this.

Direct mail—cold. Create a target list of businesses you would like to have as clients and create a series of postcards (at least 6x9") or letters with information that will help them and give them an offer that is too good to be true. It has to be a great offer for this reason: People are creatures of habit. If an Italian restaurant sent you a coupon for 10% off, would that make you not go to the Italian restaurant you have been going to for years? What if that offer was 25%? 50%? The better the offer, the higher the response rate.

○ I need more of this.

Direct mail—mailers. There are lots of companies that will deliver your product ad directly into a geographic area. These "shoppers" are designed to go into every mail box in specific zip codes. The larger the ad, the better the chance for a good response. The more times you run, the better it will work.

○ I need more of this.

Direct mail—warm. Similar to sending articles to clients, sending offers to your clients on a monthly basis is a way of staying in front of them. Make it a very special offer and include information they can use in their business. I prefer to use large postcards for this than envelopes because they are less expensive and will always be seen. You may want to split up your list and give them different offers to see which ones pull best. This is called doing an A/B split where only one thing is different. The A/B can also be a headline change.

○ I need more of this.

E-mail blasts to cold call. If you are going to buy e-mail lists and blast out to hundreds of thousands of people in the hope of selling your product, know that this requires skill to get people to open your e-mail. The subject line is most important for an open rate and your offer should be incredibly desirable. I suggest you also do lots of A/B testing to see what works best.

○ I need more of this.

E-mail blasts to customers. This is an inexpensive way to stay in touch with clients. Be certain you have your client's permission to add them to your marketing list. Give them great content and special customer-only specials.

◯ I need more of this.

Focus groups. Similar to surveys, this is when you are compensating people to sit in a room and answer questions about your product, service, advertisements, or any other message you want to try out prior to letting it out into the world. The questions you ask and the way you ask them are very important so make sure you hire someone experienced to run the groups for you.

◯ I need more of this.

Gift with purchase. One of the best ways that make-up companies market themselves is the GWP (gift with purchase) offer. Buy X dollars of product and get a free bag to carry them in. Banks used to offer toasters if you opened an account. Find the gifts that resonate with your clients and go for it. I would suggest that you use promotional products for this, since it will carry your logo and be a constant reminder of your good will.

◯ I need more of this.

Give away your service. From time to time, I will stand up at one of the networking meetings I attend and say that I will donate my time to a grass-roots non-profit that needs marketing assistance. There are certain requirements (board size, have to be currently operating—not just an idea, certain systems in place) but I am quite willing to give back. I am here to tell you that when you give away, you do get back.

◯ I need more of this.

Hard networking groups. There are dozens of these groups, the most famous being LeTip and BNI (Business Network Internationl). Only one business type per category is allowed in. Make sure you visit at least three times prior to joining so you get a strong feel for the group. Groups need to be at least thirty members in size before the number of leads takes a large leap. If it is under twenty, do not under any circumstances join. There would be a lot of work on your part to build the group instead of building your business. With membership and monthly costs, this is an investment of between $1000 and $2500 a year.

◯ I need more of this.

Have a radio show. You can be on the radio! It is a lot easier than you think.

This is a fun way to market your business. Look for my show, The Marketing Checklist, Tuesday afternoons at 4 p.m. PST. The link is at www.TheMarketingChecklist.com. We have guests that talk about their marketing trials and tribulations and successes!

○ I need more of this.

Have a television show. There are lots of cable channels that sell infomercial time. To produce a thirty-minute television show (an infomercial) can cost $5000 to $10,000. Then depending upon when your show runs, it can cost as little as $150 per cable station, depending on the geographic area, to run that show over and over again. If your script is strong enough and your offer good enough, the average cost per run becomes very low.

○ I need more of this.

Informational CD. There is a traditional method of giving out information called the brochure. By making it electronic, you are able to include video explanations of your service and other more dynamic presentations, including testimonials.

○ I need more of this.

Interview your clients on Google Hangouts. Google Hangouts are the Google equivalent of Skype. By creating a five-minute video where your customer is the star and you are just asking them questions, you will get added exposure on the Internet. We interview clients and when you search their name on the Internet, our video pops up right at the top. As of this writing, Google has still kept the use of GHOs as a free service because they own YouTube and GHOs create additional content for that other website.

○ I need more of this.

Invoice stuffers. Your monthly invoice is a negative. Turn it into a more positive situation by including an information-packed flyer, or perhaps a coupon. We have one client who includes a $2 gift certificate to a local ice cream parlor.

○ I need more of this.

Landing page URL. It's easy to add web pages that are not the front page of your website, but it's where people start. You can use these "hidden" pages to direct specific target markets for special sales or for information designed only for them. They are set like this www.OurMarketingGuy. com/TipsBookSpecialNumber. You might want to go to that webpage to collect your special offer. The only way you can get to that page is by typing

it in, because there are no buttons which will direct you there.
○ I need more of this.

Magazines. Unless you have money to burn, this is a hard way to market. You would have to run large ads consistently with a great offer in the ad. There are situations where you will know your target market is reading a particular magazine and it could be a good idea. For example, if your target market is nuclear physicists, then you might want to advertise in *Nuclear Physicists Monthly Gazette*.
○ I need more of this.

Meetup groups. If your target market folk meet to do what they do together, you will find them on MeetUp.com. Become the unusual person in the usual place. One friend who sells long-term care, does this and when people ask why she is there, she says, "I have clients who have to know a lot about photographing flowers, to I am here to learn . . . not sell you insurance." The best way to work with MeetUp is to become the administrator of some of the groups you belong to. That number is limited, but you get to manage the flow of information and to plan when the meetings will happen.
○ I need more of this.

Mobile application (or app). The purpose of social media is to get people to your website where sales are made. In addition to social media, mobile apps are a way to promote your company through portable devices or smart phones. The more useful the information you put on your app, the better. An example of this is from my local chamber of commerce; you can get easy access to the member directory, event locations, and the discount program offered by members.
○ I need more of this.

Movie theater screens. Captive audiences excite you? Here is a good way to advertise. Don't just make it an ad, though. Make it interactive. Ask challenging questions that will cause discussion. The human mind hates an unanswered question! Did you know that? Did you just answer that question? Do you want me to stop asking questions? See how that will work? In addition to a question, offer a huge special if they text a message to your auto responder. This is great for retail businesses and restaurants which are local to the theater. It will build your list of local residents.
○ I need more of this.

Network with businesses selling a different product to the same market. There are lots of companies who share the same customers. Electricians, painters, and plumbers. Photographers, bakers and videographers. Insurance salespeople, accountants, financial planners and bankers. Get to know them and get used to sending them business. It will make you look good to your clients and make you the go-to person for what they need. I have networked with printers, graphic artists, various salespeople for different advertising methods and even other marketing professionals.
○ I need more of this.

Newsletter. Still an awesome way of staying in monthly touch with clients and your targeted markets. It does not have to be completely about your company or industry. Consider making it like the *Reader's Digest*, touching many subjects. Whether you send it electronically or through the mail (a better way) *always* send it on the same day of the month.
○ I need more of this.

Newspaper ads. As readership drops, most of the time, newspapers are offering online versions of their product to go along with the newsprint. Consistency is important, as well as the days you run it, ad size, and the offer you put into the ad. If there is a newspaper that targets your market, this is probably a good buy. Best example: Your local college newspaper if the students of that school are your target.
○ I need more of this.

Open houses at your factory. If you have a factory or something goes on in your company that is visually interesting, offer open houses to your clients and potential clients. This is a way of giving detailed information on what may be a complicated process to a captive audience. In the promotional products industry, many of our factories do this so they can explain how they imprint products so that those of us who sell the products can better explain them to our end users. By allowing a mix of current clients to network with people you want as clients, you are letting them give you lots of social proof.
○ I need more of this.

Pay-per-click ads. If you have a limited budget and can strongly determine your target market, PPC ads can bring you more business. This type of marketing is an art form in itself so proceed cautiously. Your headline must be incredibly strong. *Warning: make sure you put a daily limit on the amount you can* *spend on any one day.* Start low and work your way up as you see the results. A/B testing here is vital.

◯ I need more of this.

Press releases. The old saying "untold is unsold" applies here. Be a regular sender of releases to your local media. It does not have to do with anything that your company is doing, though that would be good. It can also be what your company officially thinks about something that is going on that relates to your industry.

◯ I need more of this.

Promotional products. I have been a proud distributor of promotional products for over thirty years. That's because they are the only advertising that people like to receive. I have always been amazed by what people will do if you promise them a free t-shirt. If you have the right promotional products professional, they will do far more than just hand you a catalog. Have the rep find the most useful and needed products for your various target markets. These promotional products will stay behind you as silent salespeople, sharing your message for more often than you can. Promotional products are not a one-size-fits-all type of advertising. Different targets will require different products. As an example, companies like using pens. But what kind? Are they nicer pens for specific targeted clients? Or are they less expensive pens that are used for mass distribution when you are cold calling or go to trade shows.

◯ I need more of this.

Public Relations. This is the art of telling your story through the press. It is capturing attention in a positive way so that your target market wants to hear what you have to say. For example: My chamber of commerce decided to have its largest family event, a street fair without alcohol. We decided that for the profits we forfeited, we would get more benefits by eschewing beer, wine, and cocktails. We sent press releases out that named our sponsors full support for our decision and that made them all say they wanted to sponsor again the next year. That lowered our sales cost!

◯ I need more of this.

Public speaking. Are you speaking to groups? It is a fantastic way to position yourself as the expert in your field. You have the social-proof backing of the organization that puts you on stage and allows you to, in effect, make a one on one presentation to ten, twenty, or hundreds of potential clients at a time.

If you are shy, Toastmasters is a great group to join to develop your speaking skills. Important tip: Always video yourself speaking. This is great content for your Youtube channel and will allow your potential clients to get to know you prior to them even meeting with you in a hiring interview. Rotary, Kiwanis, chambers of commerce and other groups constantly need speakers to bring information to their membership.

○ I need more of this.

Radio ads. For a large geographic area with a specific age range, this can be a great way to promote. You may want to consider being the big fish on a smaller station in your market. This way you can always bargain for the best rates. Let the radio station do the production of your ads. They are experts over the airwaves. You will have to be a consistent advertiser for at least three months for this to begin to gather steam. If you want to try radio, contact us for an ad on my show, The Marketing Checklist. Mention this book special and you will get 15% off our published rates.

○ I need more of this.

Referral system. We discussed previously that there are three ways to get more business. Since the most expensive way is to get new clients, let's cut that cost down by developing a system of rewards for referrals. It can be discounted product, special services, or really cool promotional product gifts that you purchase for them with *their* name on them, but find something that relates to your clients so they will self-incentivize to market *you*.

○ I need more of this.

Shock and awe kit. When someone asks for "some information" about your business, this kit is designed to attract attention and be so filled with customer-oriented content that it clearly positions you in a positive position compared to your competition. The checklist for an S&A kit includes sections on packaging (how its delivered can be most important), sales information (trial offer form, guarantee certificate, services brochure, FAQ, thank you note), proof and credibility content (books and articles you've written, testimonials, endorsements) , and attention grabbers (promo products and laminated tip sheets).

○ I need more of this.

Social and service groups. There are lots of networking groups where it is social first, business second. Finding them is a bit more difficult (they could be open to members of a particular religious organization for example) but could be well worth it. Some of these are Rotary and Kiwanis.

○ I need more of this.

Soft networking groups. I am a poster boy for chamber of congress memberships. If only to support the community, find some great vendors and be involved with local politics, chambers are a civic duty. But then when you add the ability to do *lots* of business, this is a great marketing tool . . . if you show up.

○ I need more of this.

Sponsor a team. Service companies, restaurants, or other companies that want to be seen as investing in the local community use team sponsorships as an inexpensive way to be involved. The benefit is that though this is exposure to a small group, it is for a several-month period.

○ I need more of this.

Sponsor an event. There are hundreds of events every month that are looking for sponsors. This will get you more publicity than sponsoring a local sports team, and you also get a larger audience. If you are approached and the only benefit they can give you is "It gets your name out there," *run*! If, however they give you an opportunity to speak to a large crowd, consider it.

○ I need more of this.

STAMPS.com with your photo. You can get your photo put on stamps. It's a nice extra touch for your mailings.

○ I need more of this.

Survey marketing. In the public relations courses I took in college, we were taught to create surveys. There are two ways you can use them. One is to make certain the questions go down the middle and do not push the answers toward the positive or negative. That is the harder method. The other is to stilt the questions toward the direction you want them to go. These are used if you send the survey to past clients that you want back. Take full responsibility for doing something wrong, invite them back, give them the survey that shines brightly on you, and give them a special offer to come back.

○ I need more of this.

Television. You know there are dozens of cable television channels. It costs a bit to create the ads, but the ads can be very inexpensive if you pick your cable

channels carefully. Targeting men eighteen to thirty-five? Buy the ESPN and FOX Sports channels. No reason to buy the Cooking channel.
○ I need more of this.

Testimonials. Giving and getting *video* testimonials is one of the best marketing tools. You want to have them on your website and link them back to the person who gives it to you. You want to become an expert at giving them to people so your name appears on their website.
○ I need more of this.

Texts— just saying hello. Waiting for a movie to start? In line at the bank? Pull out your cell phone and send a couple of clients a text that says, "Hey, I was thinking about you. Hope you are having a great day." This is a simple way to strengthen relationships with clients that will take very little time.
○ I need more of this.

Text marketing. Offering a discount or free information if you text a code word to a specific number on a smart phone is a great way to build a data base. Here is how it can work: At a local ballpark, we are given the opportunity to win a prize by answering a question on the scoreboard. Later on, we receive discount specials from the restaurant chain that sponsored the scoreboard promotion. On a smaller scale, a business can put a flyer on the counter that offers a discount if the customer texts a code to a number. They are sent an immediate text that they show to the cashier who reduces their price. This develops a list of paying clients who are fans of getting discount messages from your company.
○ I need more of this.

Trade shows. I am a Tradeshowaholic. If the people going by your booth or table are one of your prime demographic targets, that is incredible. Figure out in advance what your break even number is (My rough equation is cost of booth + employee time + giveaways + printing + travel x 3 = break even number) and if you can beat it easily with sales, go for it.
○ I need more of this.

Video. The camera is your friend. More video equals more money. Speaking to groups, testimonials, showing how you do the things people pay you for (a restaurant showing how their favorite dish is prepared, a handyman describ-

ing how to hang a door) is more than likely going to get you more business. The people who want to do it themselves, were never going to be your clients!
○ I need more of this.

Volunteer opportunities. Give back. It makes you feel good and when you find a way to give back that speaks to you, you will meet other, like-minded people. Who do people like to do business with? People they like that are like them. Do not go into giving of your time with this mindset, but be aware that it could happen.
○ I need more of this.

Website. A *good* website is where the magic happens. Your clients are going to connect with you so make it reflect your company's personality. What saddens me most is when I see a client's website that is not all it can be. Your site should be updated constantly with data and be evaluated for an overhaul every twenty-four to forty-eight months. Just A SIDE NOTE - On a Wordpress site, there is a plugin called Pretty Link that allows you to take a very long URL and turn it in to a very short link that most people are more apt to click on..
○ I need more of this.

Website blogging. We discussed this earlier, so consider this a strong reminder. You need to be adding to your website on a constant basis. You can also ask other business owners to guest blog on your website. They will link that blog back to their website and you will get additional viewers.
○ I need more of this.

Workshops—lunch. A lunch and learn can be set up in your office for several of your own clients and prospects or you can be the expert speaker that one of your clients brings in to educate their clients. This makes you look good to your clients and solidifies your relationship with them.
○ I need more of this.

Workshops—1,2,3 days. These take a lot of work to put together but can be an awesome way to market yourself. Consider hiring an event planner to assist you. Helpful hints: Do *not* make them free because people will get more out of a workshop they paid for. Fill them with content but do *not* make them constant "pitch fests" designed mostly to sell other services. Yes, you will make an offer, but do not make your guests feel like they are sitting in a time share presentation.

◯ I need more of this.

Write a book. The first six letters of the word Authority are *author*. I am not asking for you to re-write *War and Peace*, just get your thoughts down on paper. This book does not contain everything in my brain about marketing, but I hope you have gotten much more value than you expected. What stops most people is that they say, "I could never write a book." Read the last chapter of this book and you will see that it is easier than you think.

◯ I need more of this.

Yellow Page (offline/online). Traditionally, this was where brick and mortar and service businesses *had* to advertise to be seen. Then enter the Internet and search engines with location key words. *Now*, the main Yellow Page service offers their own search engine and web services. I think I would pass here. *Warning*: If you search for your name on the Internet and listings on yellow page-type websites come up above your own website, you have a *huge* problem with your website being found.

◯ I need more of this.

Did you enjoy this list?

Do you want more marketing ideas?

Come to OurMarketingGuy.com/MoreIdeas for a free report of ideas that are not in the book. As I come up with them, they will just be added! If you have tactics that you use which are not on this list come to the site and let us know what they are.

"People now feel time accelerating.
Lists allow them to feel some sense of accomplishment."
David Viscott

77

How Are You Marketing Your Company?

Use this chapter to list all the ways you are using to market your company. Use your notes from the list in the previous chapter to help complete the list of your current market strategy. There might be things that you did not even realize you were doing ("I go to my chamber lunch every month, I didn't even think of that as marketing.").

After you have made the list, go back and give a letter grade to each tool on your list. The reason you will not grade them as you go, is because I want you to be able to compare each of them as you go through the exercise. This will put your methods on a curve and let you compare them against the rest of the "class." The grade can be based on anything you wish (revenue, fun, leads) but be very honest with yourself. The more honest the grade, the better this list will serve you. You may want to have more than one person in your organization perform this task and then compare lists.

Things to keep in mind as you assign a grade:

- *Sales*—is the tactic leading you to sales? What percentage of your total sales can you attribute to it?

- *Referrals*—is the tactic leading you to referrals from other clients?

- *Attendance*—does the marketing tactic "show up" to work all the time?

- *Ease of use*—are your "dollars realized" divided by "hours per sale" a high number compared to the other tactics?

- *Cost per sale*—How is the ratio of "dollars realized" divided by "dollars spent" (including labor) compared to other tactics? Note—cold calling is going to have an out-of-whack number, but that should not be a factor here. It is the quality of the cold calls that should be evaluated.

Okay, time for you to do some of the work and let my fingers rest for a bit.

Marketing Tactic   Grade

		Grade
1.		
2.		
3.		
4.		
5.		
6.		
7.		
8.		
9.		
10.		

Add more as needed!

Now note which new ideas you would like to try:

1. _____

2. _____

3. _____

4. _____

5. _____

We follow the marketing axiom that the more legs to our marketing stool, the more stable the sales function of our company.
○ YES   ○ NO

"True genius resides in the capacity for evaluation of uncertain, hazardous and conflicting information."
Winston Churchill

78

Evaluate Your Current Marketing Tactics

Now that you have gone through the list and graded each item, let's put those grades to work.

Any tactics that get lower than a "C" (that includes "C-") grade goes. You do not currently have the resources to continue them. Any that got a "C" are on probation.

The question to ask is, "Will getting help from an outside source help move this to a B or an A?" It might be that your blogging is only getting a "C" because you are not blogging often enough or you do not consider yourself a good writer. Hiring someone to write your blogs would inexpensively improve this to a higher grade and you should do it. Perhaps your "in person networking" is weak because you are not able to get to the groups meetings often enough. Is there someone on your staff that you can train to do that? We have been hired to do social media posting for companies and improved their responses instantly. We have also run birthday programs, surveys, create successful direct mail programs, and Shock and Awe kits. Let someone take the pressure off you while you do what you do best!

If it got a "B," is there an *easy* way to improve them to an "A"? That should be where you spend more time and effort. It is the best way to capture more business. Maybe adding another trade show to your marketing calendar will increase the number of leads your salespeople can follow up with. Perhaps you need to find ways to increase your e-mail list so that you can be more effective with your e-mail blasts.

If it got an "A", keep using it at the level you are currently unless you can decrease the dollars you spend there and still get an "A". Let's say you were holding open houses at your factory every month and it was giving you great results. Can you do it ten times a year and have the same results?

Just like every semester you got a report card in school, keep up this process of grading your marketing tactics until you improve the Grade Point Average of your marketing.

If you want a bit of help, the team at WeLove@OurMarketingGuy.com is willing to give you a quick-look evaluation as a thank you for buying this book. Send your list from the previous chapter in PDF form to

QuickLookEvalution@OurMarketingGuy.com. Include your name, company name, web address, approximate yearly sales, and the approximate amount of your yearly marketing budget.

Evaluating our marketing was an easy task. It is a task we will do often.
◯ YES   ◯ NO

---

*"Feelings are more dangerous than ideas, because they aren't
susceptible to rational evaluation. They grow quietly,
spreading underground, and erupt suddenly, all over the place."*
Brian Eno

79

Balance Is Beautiful

As we are taught in our personal investment strategies, you should strive for a balance in your marketing tactics. Methods which are bringing in lots of sales, will not always continue to work. By having a very diverse strategy, your sales will increase. As you have been reading this book, you have already begun making a list of changes that should occur on your marketing checklist. You will want to make a separate checklist of just the "no"s to see where you need to shore up your marketing. It may be that only a few of them need to be corrected, but knowing which methods need a change in course is vital to your overall success. If you need some help creating this balance, get hold of my team at our website, www.OurMarketingGuy.com.

"Balance, peace, and joy are the fruit of a successful life.
It starts with recognizing your talents
and finding ways to serve others by using them."
Thomas Kinkade

80

Why Am I Writing A Book?
One Little Last Bit of Truth in Marketing

As a marketer by college education and thirty plus years of practical experience in the field, I have had the opportunity to use dozens of different tools to market myself. I love using promotional products of all kinds (motivational calendars, pens, and cowbells are three of my favorites), but in this last chapter I want to talk about a relatively new addition to that list: my books.

When I first began to use books as an expanded brochure, I noticed three things. First, just like when we blog we are only looking for three to five hundred words, with a book, we are not looking for *Great Expectations*. A book of this size that runs between sixty-four and 128 pages (it is less expensive to print books in multiples of sixteen pages) is a relatively easy target to hit if you have help getting focused. Second, not many people in my industry had ever thought of producing a book, let alone getting one published. I would bet it is the same for you. If you are an expert it will not be hard, if you have the desire. One way to do it is to take fifty of your favorite blog posts and repurpose them into a book. About a third of this book was written that way. The third thing is that when I give out the book, it generates a lot of buzz. When we put together marketing plans for clients we want to generate buzz, so this is a good tool.

The reason is that you put a lot of your expertise into a book for your potential clients to read. When we put together marketing plans for clients and they decide to take our advice to become an author, we help them create their entire book as a content-filled sales tool.

This is an important note: The best promotional products are *useful* and *needed* by the target market. If you are going to use your books as a sales tool, remember that they must be filled with great content that will be useful and needed by your target market. You will want to pull the curtain back and give your readers so much great information that you are set *way* apart from competitors. It's the reason I am putting this chapter last, so I can use it as an easy-to-find description of what Our Marketing Guy does for its clients.

Books as a promotional product? When you talk to potential clients, one of the greatest factors in being hired is to be seen as an authority in the field. In the self-publishing world, you can create a thousand books for about

$4,500 (do not hold me to this—my first book, *49 Stupid Things People Do with Business Cards . . . and How to Fix Them* cost a lot more because almost every page is in full color). In the promotional products industry, to find a great product that does what a book can do, share your message in long form, for that price it is pretty awesome.

There are lots of ways to chart out your book and what you are going to put into it. A little research on the Internet will give you many different methods to follow. I also found a cool website called WritersDigest.com. They offer a free yearly report on the one hundred best websites for writers. You can also, of course, get in touch with us at OurMarketingGuy.com and we will connect you with our team (cover artists, editors, printing companies, publishers).

On that note, thank you for reading this book. I hope you have gotten a lot out of it. If you have some important marketing questions, head to our website, OurMarketingGuy.com and submit it on our marketing questions page.

Life requires business.

Business requires marketing.

Marketing is education.

Education creates value.

Value is the only thing that sells.

Sales is service.

Service is a noble thing.

What pain do you remove from your customer? That is what they are paying you for.

To help remove some of your pain, there is an "I bought your book" bonus on the next page.

167

Made in the USA
San Bernardino, CA
28 July 2015